delicious.
MAGAZINE

WICKED DESSERTS

D1513873

HarperCollins*Publishers*
77–85 Fulham Palace Road,
Hammersmith, London W6 8JB
www.harpercollins.co.uk

First published by HarperCollins*Publishers* 2009

10 9 8 7 6 5 4 3 2

© Seven Publishing Group Ltd 2009

A catalogue record of this book is available from the British Library

ISBN-13   978-0-00-729256-1

Printed and bound in China by South China Printing Co.

delicious. MAGAZINE
WICKED DESSERTS

Edited by Debbie Major

Magazine Editor
Matthew Drennan

HarperCollins*Publishers*

contents

introduction

The one thing I often find disappointing with desserts on restaurant menus, and indeed in some cookery books, is a lack of imagination. It's often a collection of what I call the usual suspects: crème brulée, vanilla panna cotta, apple pie – you get the picture. But what I really love about this brilliant collection of puddings in **delicious. wicked desserts** is how original and clever they are, offering unusual twists on classics such as white chocolate and pistachio panna cotta, or spiced pear and ginger jellies, or baked gooseberry and crème fraiche cheesecake.

'Wicked' is a regular long-running series in **delicious.** magazine that is unashamedly luxurious and divine; but that doesn't mean recipes that are complicated or overly fussy. With some ingenious know-how and clever ideas the cookery team here at **delicious.** HQ have put together their best creations from chocolate desserts to fruity puddings, from ices, ice-cream and sorbets to creamy desserts and mousses. Just don't count the calories!

All the recipes have been tried and tested in the **delicious.** test kitchen until we are satisfied that they will read, cook and taste to the highest standards.

Matthew Drennan
delicious. Magazine Editor

Conversion tables

All the recipes in this book list only metric measurements (also used by Australian cooks). The conversions listed here are approximate for imperial measurements (also used by American cooks).

Oven temperatures

°C	Fan°C	°F	Gas	Description
110	90	225	¼	Very cool
120	100	250	½	Very cool
140	120	275	1	Cool
150	130	300	2	Cool
160	140	325	3	Warm
180	160	350	4	Moderate
190	170	375	5	Moderately hot
200	180	400	6	Fairly hot
220	200	425	7	Hot
230	210	450	8	Very hot
240	220	475	9	Very hot

Weights for dry ingredients

Metric	Imperial	Metric	Imperial
7g	¼oz	425g	15oz
15g	½oz	450g	1lb
20g	¾oz	500g	1lb 2oz
25g	1oz	550g	1¼lb
40g	1½oz	600g	1lb 5oz
50g	2oz	650g	1lb 7oz
60g	2½oz	675g	1½lb
75g	3oz	700g	1lb 9oz
100g	3½oz	750g	1lb 11oz
125g	4oz	800g	1¾lb
140g	4½oz	900g	2lb
150g	5oz	1kg	2¼lb
165g	5½oz	1.1kg	2½lb
175g	6oz	1.25kg	2¾lb
200g	7oz	1.35kg	3lb
225g	8oz	1.5kg	3lb 6oz
250g	9oz	1.8kg	4lb
275g	10oz	2kg	4½lb
300g	11oz	2.25kg	5lb
350g	12oz	2.5kg	5½lb
375g	13oz	2.75kg	6lb
400g	14oz	3kg	6¾lb

Liquid measures

Metric	Imperial	Aus	US
25ml	1fl oz		
50ml	2fl oz	¼ cup	¼ cup
75ml	3fl oz		
100ml	3½fl oz		
120ml	4fl oz	½ cup	½ cup
150ml	5fl oz		
175ml	6 fl oz	¾ cup	¾ cup
200ml	7fl oz		
250ml	8fl oz	1 cup	1 cup
300ml	10fl oz/½ pint	½ pint	1¼ cups
360ml	12fl oz		
400ml	14fl oz		
450ml	15fl oz	2 cups	2 cups/1 pint
600ml	1 pint	1 pint	2½ cups
750ml	1¼ pints		
900ml	1½ pints		
1 litre	1¾ pints	1¾ pints	1 quart
1.2 litres	2 pints		
1.4 litres	2½ pints		
1.5 litres	2¾ pints		
1.7 litres	3 pints		
2 litres	3½ pints		
3 litres	5¼ pints		

UK–Australian tablespoon conversions

1 x UK or Australian teaspoon is 5ml

1 x UK tablespoon is 3 teaspoons/15ml

1 Australian tablespoon is 4 teaspoons/20ml

chocolate

Orange, almond and chocolate dessert cake

For a decadent treat, try this moist orange cake covered with chocolate ganache. Serve with scoops of crème fraîche.

SERVES 12
TAKES 2½ HOURS, PLUS COOLING

2 oranges
150g plain chocolate, broken
  into pieces
5 eggs
400g golden caster sugar
350g sunflower oil
125g ground almonds
25g cocoa powder
375g plain flour
1½ tsp baking powder
3–4 tbsp orange liqueur, such
  as Cointreau or Grand Marnier

For the topping:
350g plain chocolate, broken
  into pieces
225ml double cream
Crystallised orange peel,
  to decorate

1. Simmer the oranges in a pan of water for 30 minutes. Drain, then whiz to a purée in a food processor. Cool.

2. Meanwhile, preheat the oven to 180°C/fan 160°C/gas 4. Grease and base line a deep, 23–24cm round cake tin. Melt the chocolate in a bowl set over a pan of simmering water. Remove from the heat, stir until smooth, then cool.

3. In a large bowl, lightly beat together the eggs, sugar and oil. Gradually beat in the orange purée, then the chocolate. Sift in the almonds, cocoa, flour and baking powder, and fold in. Spoon the mixture into the tin and bake for 1 hour 20 minutes (cover with foil if it gets too brown), or until a skewer inserted into the centre comes out clean. Invert the tin to remove the cake, so its base is now uppermost, and cool on a rack. Then drizzle the base with the liqueur.

4. For the topping, melt the chocolate as above. Remove from the heat and stir in the cream. Cool until thick enough to spread, stirring occasionally. Swirl over the cake and decorate with crystallised orange peel.

St-Emilion au chocolat torte

A new twist on a French classic. Macaroons are usually soaked in brandy, but here tiny Italian ratafias are soaked in amaretto liqueur for a deep almond flavour.

SERVES 8

TAKES 40 MINUTES, 40 MINUTES TO BAKE, PLUS CHILLING AND COOLING

375g sweet shortcrust pastry

250g plain chocolate (no less than 70% cocoa solids), broken into pieces

250ml double cream

2 eggs, separated

5 tbsp caster sugar

75g ratafias (small, round Italian biscuits)

2½ tbsp amaretto liqueur

Chocolate curls, to decorate

Cocoa powder, for dusting

1. Preheat the oven to 200°C/fan 180°C/gas 6. Thinly roll out the pastry and use to line a 4cm-deep, round, fluted 23cm tart tin. Line with baking paper and baking beans, and bake for 20 minutes. Remove the beans and paper, brush the base with a little of the egg white and bake for another 5 minutes. Remove and reduce the oven temperature to 140°C/fan 120°C/gas 1.

2. Melt the chocolate and cream in a bowl over a pan of simmering water. Leave to cool for 15 minutes.

3. Whisk the egg whites in a clean bowl to soft peaks, then whisk in 2 tablespoons of the caster sugar. In another bowl, whisk the egg yolks and remaining sugar together until thick and creamy. Stir in the chocolate mixture, then fold in the meringue.

4. Spread a little filling in the pastry case. Toss 8 ratafias at a time in the amaretto, drain off the excess and arrange on top. Pour over the remaining filling and bake for 15 minutes. Remove from the oven, and leave to cool. Then top with chocolate curls and dust with cocoa powder.

This will keep in the fridge for up to 3 days. Serve at room temperature with lightly whipped cream.

Variation If you like the flavour of orange with chocolate, soak the ratafias in an orange-flavoured liqueur, such as Grand Marnier, instead.

Nutty chocolate meringues

Once these are filled with cream, either eat them straight away if you prefer them crispy, or up to 4 hours later for a more squidgy experience.

MAKES 12

TAKES 35 MINUTES, 40 MINUTES TO BAKE, PLUS FREEZING AND COOLING

100g piece good-quality plain chocolate (70% cocoa solids)
3 large egg whites
Pinch of cream of tartar
125g caster sugar
50g icing sugar, sifted
1 tsp cocoa powder, sifted
30g toasted hazelnuts, finely ground
142ml carton double cream

1. Freeze the chocolate for 30 minutes. Meanwhile, preheat the oven to 140°C/fan 120°C/gas 1. Line two large baking sheets with baking paper.

2. Finely grate 50g of frozen chocolate into a bowl. Return to the freezer until needed. Break the remainder into another bowl and set aside.

3. Whisk the egg whites and cream of tartar into stiff peaks in a clean bowl. Gradually whisk in the caster sugar to make a thick, glossy meringue. Sift over and fold in the icing sugar in three batches.

4. Mix the cocoa, hazelnuts and grated chocolate together. Fold gently into the meringue. Spoon into a piping bag fitted with a 1.5cm fluted nozzle, and pipe 24 spiralled peaks on to the baking sheets, well spaced apart. Bake for 40 minutes until firm. Remove from the oven and leave to cool.

5. Melt the remaining chocolate in a bowl over simmering water. Spread some of the chocolate on to the base of each meringue and leave to set, chocolate-side up.

6. Whip the cream into soft peaks. Sandwich the meringues together with the cream and serve.

★DELICIOUS. TIP The secret is to make sure the meringue mixture is quite stiff at all stages. If small bubbles start to appear during baking, reduce the oven heat to 120°C/fan 100°C/gas ½.

Variation Use toasted blanched almonds instead of hazelnuts, if you prefer.

Chocolate and prune galettes

This French chocolate recipe looks very smart but is so simple to make – and the prunes will do you good, too.

MAKES 8
TAKES 40 MINUTES, PLUS SETTING

150g plain chocolate (at least 70% cocoa solids), broken into pieces

200g dried ready-to-eat prunes, finely chopped

2 tbsp Armagnac or brandy

2 tbsp icing sugar, plus extra for dusting

500ml double cream

24 crystallised violets, to decorate

1. Line a board with baking paper. Melt the chocolate in a heatproof bowl over a pan of simmering water, stir until smooth, then pour on to the paper and spread out thinly into a rectangle measuring 36cm x 24cm. Leave to set.

2. Dip a long, sharp knife in boiling water. Cut the chocolate into 24 x 6cm squares, drying the knife and re-dipping in the water each time you make a cut.

3. Put the prunes, Armagnac and icing sugar into a food processor and blend until smooth. Stir in 150ml of the cream. Press through a sieve into a bowl and stir in the remaining cream. Beat until stiff enough to pipe. Spoon into a piping bag fitted with a 1.5cm plain nozzle.

4. Pipe a generous amount of the prune mixture on to 8 chocolate squares, top with another square and repeat. Place on a baking sheet, in two neat rows of 4, and chill if the chocolate is soft.

5. Cut 4 long, 5mm wide, strips of baking paper. Lay evenly spaced over the galettes and sift over some icing sugar. Carefully remove the paper. Decorate with crystallised violets and serve.

★DELICIOUS. TIP If you wish to make the chocolate squares in advance, layer them up in an airtight container between squares of baking paper. They will keep for 2 days.

White chocolate and pistachio panna cottas

This delicious recipe is made even richer with the addition of vanilla-scented white chocolate and flavoursome pistachios.

MAKES 4

TAKES 25 MINUTES, PLUS 2 HOURS SETTING

568ml carton double cream
2 tbsp caster sugar
2½ sheets leaf gelatine
150g good-quality white chocolate, finely chopped
50g shelled pistachio nuts
Dark chocolate thins, to decorate
Crystallised rose petals, to decorate

1. Put the cream and sugar in a pan over a medium heat. As soon as bubbles appear, turn the heat down to very low and cook for 12 minutes.

2. Meanwhile, soak the gelatine in a bowl of cold water for 5 minutes.

3. Add the chocolate to the hot cream and stir until smooth. Lift the gelatine out of the water (no need to squeeze it), and stir into the hot mixture to dissolve. Remove from the heat.

4. Grind the pistachios finely in a mini processor or clean coffee grinder. Add to the cream mixture and allow to infuse for 15 minutes. Pass through a sieve into a jug, then divide among 4 x 150ml dariole moulds or ramekins. Chill for 2 hours, until set.

5. To turn out, dip the bases of the moulds very briefly in hot water, then invert on to serving plates. Decorate with the chocolate thins and a few crystallised rose petals.

★DELICIOUS. TIP Use any dark chocolates to decorate, but make sure they are thin and not too large so that they balance the dish. Top with any sugared decoration that will complement the creamy green colour of the panna cottas.

Chocolate cheesecake ice cream biscuits

Not all ice creams need constant whisking to keep them smooth; the dense cream cheese here doesn't need whipping.

SERVES 6

TAKES 20 MINUTES, PLUS CHILLING, 4 HOURS FREEZING AND 5 MINUTES SETTING

300g plain chocolate, broken into pieces

500g tub ready-made fresh vanilla custard

400g tub light cream cheese

100g icing sugar, sifted

100ml milk, chilled

12 chocolate or chocolate chip digestive biscuits, to serve

1. Melt 200g of the chocolate with the custard in a heatproof bowl set over a pan of simmering water, stirring until smooth.

2. Put the cream cheese and icing sugar into a large mixing bowl, and gradually whisk in the warm chocolate custard until combined. Whisk in the milk, and chill for 15 minutes.

3. Pour the mixture into a shallow plastic container (about 1.5 litres), cover and freeze for 2 hours, or until almost frozen.

4. Put the remaining chocolate into a small plastic food bag and knot the top to seal. Microwave for 1 minute to melt the chocolate (or melt in a heatproof bowl over a pan of simmering water and pour into a bag), then snip off a tiny corner of the bag. Take the ice cream out of the freezer and drizzle over the chocolate. Leave to set for 5 minutes. Then stir the set chocolate into the ice cream, breaking it into chips as you do so. Re-freeze for a further 2 hours or until completely frozen. To serve, sandwich scoops of ice cream between 2 biscuits.

Chocolate fudge pots with blueberries in cassis

This classy dessert is just perfect for summer entertaining.

SERVES 6
READY IN 20 MINUTES, PLUS 1 HOUR
CHILLING

200g plain chocolate (up to 50% cocoa solids), broken into pieces

100g unsalted butter, cut into 6 pieces

4 medium eggs, separated

150g blueberries

150ml crème de cassis (blackcurrant) liqueur

6 tbsp Greek yogurt, crème fraîche or fromage frais, to serve

1. Put the chocolate and butter into a heatproof bowl. Melt over a pan of simmering water or in a 900-watt microwave on medium for 30-second bursts, until melted. Stir well to combine.

2. Whisk the egg whites to soft peaks, then add the yolks to the chocolate mixture and mix together until smooth and glossy. Then gently fold in the whisked egg whites. Carefully spoon the mixture into 6 individual pots and chill for at least 1 hour.

3. Put the blueberries into a pan with the cassis liqueur. Just bring to the boil to soften, then remove the fruit with a slotted spoon and put in a bowl. Boil the cassis for 2–3 minutes, until reduced and syrupy. Pour over the blueberries and cool.

4. Top each chocolate fudge pot with a dollop of Greek yogurt, crème fraîche or fromage frais. Spoon over the blueberries in cassis syrup and serve.

Gooey chocolate puds with whole cherry sauce

You can prepare these in advance and chill for up to 5 hours, then bake for 9–10 minutes for centres oozing with chocolate.

SERVES 6
READY IN 35 MINUTES

50g light muscovado sugar

100g cherries, halved and stoned, plus 100g cherries, stalks left on

150ml Moscato wine

175g unsalted butter, cubed, plus extra for greasing

175g plain chocolate, broken into pieces

4 eggs, plus 4 egg yolks

75g golden caster sugar

75g plain flour, sieved

1. In a pan, dissolve the muscovado sugar in 2 tablespoons of water, then simmer until syrupy. Add the halved cherries and cook gently for 1 minute. Add the wine and simmer vigorously for 5 minutes to reduce. Add the whole cherries and cook for a further minute. Cool.

2. Preheat the oven to 190°C/fan 170°C/ gas 5. Grease 6cm x 8cm cooking rings and place on a baking sheet lined with baking paper.

3. Melt the butter and chocolate in a heatproof bowl over a pan of simmering water. Remove and set aside.

4. Whisk the eggs, egg yolks and caster sugar together with an electric mixer until very thick and moussey. Gently fold in the chocolate mixture, then the flour. Chill for 10 minutes, or until the mixture is firm.

5. Divide the mixture among the rings and bake for 8–10 minutes. Lift on to plates, remove the rings and spoon the cherry sauce over and around each pud.

★ DELICIOUS. TIP If you don't have any baking rings, use greased Yorkshire pudding tins instead.

Caramel, pecan and dark chocolate tart

Serve this very rich tart in thin wedges with a dollop of crème fraîche for dessert – there will be plenty left for afternoon tea.

SERVES 8
TAKES 20 MINUTES, PLUS 2½ HOURS CHILLING AND SETTING

75g butter
200g digestive biscuits, crushed

For the filling:
150g butter
150g unrefined light muscovado sugar
½ x 397g can condensed milk
100g good-quality plain chocolate, broken into pieces
50g pecan nuts, toasted and roughly chopped

1. Melt the butter in a pan, and stir in the crushed biscuits. Press over the base and up the sides of a 20cm loose-bottomed, fluted flan tin to make the biscuit casing. Chill for 30 minutes until set.

2. Make the filling. Put the butter and sugar into a pan over a gentle heat, and stir until dissolved. Add the condensed milk and boil over a gentle heat for 2–3 minutes, stirring continuously, to make a golden caramel. Pour into the tart case and chill for 1 hour.

3. Melt the chocolate in a heatproof bowl over a pan of simmering water, then leave to cool until slightly thickened. Spoon the chocolate into a small sandwich bag and snip off the corner. Quickly drizzle in zig-zag lines over the tart. Sprinkle the tart with the chopped pecans and leave the cake to set in a cool place for 1 hour before serving.

Rich chocolate mousse torte

This glamorous dessert is simply a rich chocolate mousse set in a chocolate biscuit crust.

SERVES 8–10

TAKES 40 MINUTES, PLUS AT LEAST 4 HOURS CHILLING

Butter for greasing
1 tsp instant coffee granules
150g plain chocolate (at least 60% cocoa solids), broken into pieces
3 large eggs, separated, plus 1 egg yolk
1 tsp vanilla extract
4 tbsp Cointreau
3 tbsp golden caster sugar

For the biscuit case:
50g plain chocolate (at least 60% cocoa solids), broken into pieces
50g butter
2 tbsp cocoa powder
175g digestive biscuits, crushed
2 tbsp golden caster sugar

1. Remove the base from a 20cm springform tin. Lightly butter inside the ring and place it upside-down on a serving plate. Secure in place with small pieces of Blu-Tack. Line the sides with baking paper.

2. Make the biscuit case. Melt the chocolate, butter and cocoa powder in a heatproof bowl over a pan of simmering water. Stir in the biscuit crumbs. Press the mixture in an even layer over the base and 4cm up the sides of the tin to form a casing. Chill.

3. Dissolve the coffee in 4 tablespoons of boiling water. Melt the chocolate with the coffee in a large heatproof bowl over a pan of simmering water. Remove the bowl from the pan and stir in the egg yolks, vanilla extract and Cointreau.

4. Whisk the egg whites in a bowl until just beginning to stiffen, then gradually whisk in the sugar to form a soft meringue. Fold into the chocolate mixture and pour into the case. Chill for 4 hours or overnight until firm, then remove the tin and serve.

Note: This recipe contains raw egg.

Variation This torte could be flavoured with any spirit of your choice: brandy, rum or amaretto liqueur would all also work well.

Chocolate and cherry ice cream sundae

This dessert has all the flavours of a classic Black Forest gateau in one glass.

SERVES 6
TAKES 15 MINUTES, PLUS 10 MINUTES COOLING

142ml carton double cream
1 tbsp icing sugar
1 tsp cocoa powder
400ml good-quality chocolate ice cream
3 chocolate muffins, broken into pieces
400g can pitted cherries, drained, but juice reserved for the sauce
Grated plain chocolate, to decorate

For the chocolate cherry caramel sauce:
200g soft brown sugar
142ml carton double cream
50g butter, cubed
100g plain chocolate
3 tbsp kirsch liqueur or brandy

1. Make the sauce. Put the sugar in a small pan with the juice from the can of cherries and 2 tablespoons of water. Stir over a low heat until the sugar has dissolved. Remove from the heat and stir in the cream, butter and chocolate until smooth, then stir in the kirsch or brandy. Cool slightly for 10 minutes.

2. Lightly whip the cream with the icing sugar and cocoa. Set aside.

3. To assemble the sundaes, put a scoop of ice cream into each glass. Sprinkle over pieces of muffin and a few cherries, then drizzle with some sauce. Repeat these layers, then top with a spoonful of the whipped cream and some grated chocolate.

Chocolate mousse

The perfect make-ahead dessert for a dinner party; a rich chocolate mousse that will never go out of fashion.

SERVES 4

TAKES 25 MINUTES, PLUS AT LEAST 3 HOURS CHILLING

3 eggs, separated
250g plain chocolate, chopped
2 tbsp brandy or rum
300ml double cream

1. In a small bowl, lightly whip the egg yolks. Melt 200g of the chocolate with the brandy or rum in a heatproof bowl set over a pan of simmering water, stirring occasionally until smooth. Remove from the heat and gradually add the beaten yolks. Fold through the cream to combine.

2. In a large, clean bowl, whisk the egg whites with an electric hand whisk into soft peaks, then fold into the chocolate mixture. Pour evenly into glasses or cups, cover with cling film and chill for at least 3 hours or until firm.

3. Chop the remaining chocolate into small shards and sprinkle over the top just before serving.

Note: This recipe contains raw egg.

Easy white chocolate cheesecake with cherry sauce

What makes this cheesecake so easy is that it uses chocolate to make it set, rather than gelatine.

SERVES 8
TAKES 25 MINUTES, PLUS AT LEAST
4½ HOURS CHILLING

150g white chocolate, broken up
250g tub mascarpone
142ml carton whipping cream

For the cherry sauce:
1 tbsp arrowroot
150ml crème de cassis
Grated zest and juice of 1 orange
500g whole cherries, stalks
  removed

For the base:
225g chocolate digestive
  biscuits, crushed
50g butter, melted and warm

1. Brush the inside of a 450g loaf tin with water and line with cling film.

2. Melt the white chocolate in a heatproof bowl over a pan of simmering water. Remove, stir until smooth, then cool slightly.

3. In a separate bowl, beat the mascarpone until softened. In another bowl, whip the cream to soft peaks. Beat the chocolate into the mascarpone, then fold in the cream. Spoon into the tin and chill for 30 minutes until slightly firm.

4. Meanwhile for the base, mix the crushed biscuits with the butter. Spoon over the cheesecake and press lightly to level. Chill for 4 hours, or until set.

5. Make the cherry sauce. Measure out 100ml of water and mix 1 tablespoon with the arrowroot to make a paste. Bring the remaining water to the boil in a pan with the cassis, orange zest and juice. Stir in the paste and simmer until clear and thick. Add the cherries and simmer for 3 minutes. Leave to cool.

6. Invert the cheesecake on to a plate (the crumbs will now form the base) and spoon over the cherry sauce. Cut into 8 slices to serve.

fruity

Orange and passion fruit salad with cardamom syrup

This would be exquisite served with scoops of cardamom ice cream or a mixture of whipped cream and Greek-style yogurt.

SERVES 4

TAKES 30 MINUTES, PLUS CHILLING

5 large oranges
75g golden caster sugar
5 cardamom pods, lightly crushed
5–6 passion fruits, halved
1–2 tbsp fresh lemon juice
1–2 tbsp orange flower water, to serve

1. Thinly pare the zest from one of the oranges using a potato peeler, making sure you get no white pith. Cut the strips into thin shreds, place in a sieve and pour a kettleful of boiling water over them. Leave to drain.

2. Place the sugar into a small pan with 4 tablespoons of water and the crushed cardamom pods. Heat slowly until the sugar melts, then boil for 2–3 minutes. Scoop the passion-fruit pulp into the syrup, add the orange-zest shreds and stir well to break up the passion fruit. Leave to cool, then add some lemon juice to taste.

3. Take a thin slice off the top and bottom of each orange, and then cut away all the skin and white pith. Cut the fruit across into thin slices. Arrange on a serving plate and spoon over the syrup. Cover and chill until ready to serve, then sprinkle with the orange flower water.

Variation For a change, flavour the syrup with 2 star anise instead of the cardamom pods; it will still taste exotic, and just as fantastic.

Plum, pistachio and rose crumbles

These are more like pistachio-stuffed grilled plums than crumbles, but they are pretty, tasty and easy to make.

SERVES 2
READY IN 15 MINUTES

6 tbsp clear honey

Finely grated zest and juice of 2 lemons

Good splash of rosewater

3 large plums, halved and stoned

100g shelled pistachio nuts

Evaporated milk or single cream, to serve

1. Preheat the grill to high. In a bowl, mix the honey, lemon zest, lemon juice and rosewater together to make a syrup. Sit the plums cut-side down in a small roasting tin and drizzle over half the syrup. Grill for 5 minutes.

2. Meanwhile, put the pistachios and remaining syrup in a processor. Whiz until the nuts are finely chopped.

3. Turn the plums and grill for a further 5 minutes. Divide the nut mixture among the plums, then grill for a further 2–3 minutes, until golden. Serve the plums and the syrupy fruit juices with evaporated milk or cream.

Gooseberry streusel cake with elderflower syrup

This amazing pudding has a touch of rustic charm about it, and it's great for feeding large numbers.

SERVES 10

TAKES ABOUT 30 MINUTES, ABOUT
1 HOUR IN THE OVEN, PLUS COOLING

600g red or green gooseberries, topped and tailed
2 tbsp elderflower cordial
300g caster sugar
400g plain flour
200g ground almonds
400g unsalted butter, chilled and cubed
75g flaked almonds
75g flaked coconut
Clotted cream, to serve

1. Preheat the oven to 190°C/fan 170°C/gas 5. Cook the gooseberries, cordial, 100g of the caster sugar and 100ml of water in a large pan over a gentle heat for 4–5 minutes, until softened slightly. Strain, reserving the juices, and leave to cool.

2. Meanwhile, whiz the flour, almonds, remaining sugar and butter together in a food processor until it resembles coarse breadcrumbs. Transfer half to a bowl, toss with the flaked almonds and coconut and set aside.

3. Line a 30cm x 23cm shallow baking tin with baking paper. Whiz the remaining crumbs again until they form a smooth dough. Press evenly into the base of the tin, leaving a rim all around. Prick the base and bake for 15 minutes. Spoon over the strained gooseberries, scatter the crumbly mixture on top and bake for 45–50 minutes, until crisp and golden. Cool slightly in the tin, then carefully remove using the paper.

4. Simmer the reserved juices in a small pan until syrupy. Cool completely.

5. Cut the cake into wedges, drizzle with the syrup and serve with clotted cream.

Cherries Jubilee

This recipe has been adapted and improved since its invention for Queen Victoria's Golden Jubilee celebration in 1887, but still tastes just as wonderful.

SERVES 4
READY IN 15 MINUTES

1 tbsp arrowroot
150ml crème de cassis
Grated zest and juice of 1 orange
500g whole cherries, stalks removed
500g good-quality vanilla ice cream

1. Measure out 100ml of water and mix 1 tablespoon of it with the arrowroot to form a smooth paste. Put the rest of the water into a pan and add the cassis, orange zest and juice. Bring to the boil and stir in the paste. Simmer, stirring, until thick and clear.

2. Add the cherries and heat gently for 3 minutes. Scoop the ice cream into bowls, spoon over some of the sauce, and serve.

★ DELICIOUS. TIP Arrowroot thickens a sauce without making it cloudy, but you could use cornflour instead.

Strawberry soup

This unusual, chilled sweet soup is a lovely, light way of finishing a summertime meal.

SERVES 6

TAKES 15 MINUTES, PLUS CHILLING

75cl bottle medium–dry rosé wine

125g caster sugar

4 tbsp summer fruit cordial (see tip)

Strip of orange zest, plus 6 extra strips to decorate

400g small strawberries

1. Pour the rosé wine into a saucepan, add the sugar, cordial and orange zest, and heat gently, stirring, until the sugar dissolves. Remove from the heat, transfer the liquid to a large bowl, cover and chill for a few hours.

2. Hull and halve the strawberries and add to the chilled soup. Ladle the strawberry soup into 6 shallow bowls and decorate each with a piece of orange zest to serve.

★ DELICIOUS. TIP Use any cordial flavoured with summer fruits for this recipe. Raspberry is particularly good, or perhaps a delicate rose- or mint-flavoured one, if you can get them.

Pear, blackberry and eau de vie flaugnarde

This needs perfectly ripe pears (see tip). If you can't find them, poach slices in a sugar syrup or sauté in butter until tender.

SERVES 4

TAKES 20 MINUTES, PLUS 30 MINUTES IN THE OVEN

3 ripe pears
150g blackberries
4 tbsp pear eau de vie (such as Poire William)
25g unsalted butter, plus extra for greasing

For the batter:
150ml milk
150ml double cream
1 tsp vanilla essence
3 eggs
125g caster sugar
50g plain flour, sifted
Icing sugar, to serve

1. Preheat the oven to 180°C/ fan 160°C/gas 4. Halve and core the pears, then cut lengthways into 5mm slices. Put immediately into a bowl with the blackberries and eau de vie, and toss together well.

2. Make the batter. Mix the milk, cream and vanilla essence together. In a large bowl, whisk the eggs, sugar and a pinch of salt together with an electric hand whisk until it triples in volume and is pale and fluffy. Fold in the flour, then add the milky mixture.

3. Butter a metal gratin dish. Using a slotted spoon, arrange the pears and blackberries in the dish and add any eau de vie left behind to the batter mixture.

4. Pour the batter on to the pear slices, dot with the butter and bake in the oven for 30 minutes, until the batter is set. Remove from the oven and set aside for 5 minutes. Sift over a little icing sugar and serve warm.

★ DELICIOUS. TIP To catch a pear when it is just ripe you need to check it every so often. Too hard and it is not ready yet; so soft that it bruises easily and it has gone too far. The flesh of a perfectly ripe pear gives just a little to the touch.

Variation Apples would also work well in this dessert, especially if partnered with calvados or brandy for a classic combination of flavours.

Spiced pear and ginger jellies

Cinnamon, coriander seeds and pistachios make this mouthwatering dessert an exotic delight.

SERVES 6

TAKES 40 MINUTES, AT LEAST 4 HOURS SETTING, PLUS COOLING

200ml Sauternes or other medium-sweet white wine

200g caster sugar

Thinly pared zest and juice of 1 orange

Juice of 2 lemons

1½ cinnamon sticks, broken into short lengths

6 whole cloves

½ tsp coriander seeds

6 ripe pears, preferably Williams or Packham

9 dried apricots, quartered

1 piece stem ginger in syrup, drained and finely chopped

4 sheets leaf gelatine

Shelled pistachio nuts, toasted and chopped, to decorate

For the vanilla cream:

200ml double cream

2 tbsp icing sugar

Seeds of 1 vanilla pod

1. Put the wine, sugar, orange zest and juice, lemon juice, cinnamon sticks, cloves, coriander seeds and 350ml of water into a large saucepan over a low heat. Bring slowly to the boil, then simmer for 3 minutes until slightly syrupy.

2. Meanwhile, peel and core the pears. Add to the syrup, cover with a circle of baking paper, then a small saucepan lid to keep them submerged, and simmer for 10–12 minutes until tender. Leave to cool in the syrup. Remove and cut into slices.

3. Divide the pears, apricots and stem ginger among 6 x 225ml glasses.

4. Strain the liquid into a measuring jug (you need 600ml, so either simmer to reduce, or make up with wine).

5. Soak the gelatine in cold water for 5 minutes, then lift out, add to the syrup and stir until dissolved. Pour into the glasses, cool, then chill for 4 hours or overnight until set.

6. Just before serving, make the vanilla cream. Whisk the cream, icing sugar and vanilla seeds together into soft peaks. Spoon on top of each jelly and decorate with the pistachios to serve.

Bramley apple pancakes with toffee sauce and yogurt

These quick pancakes are great for breakfast, but they also make a wonderful pudding with maple syrup and vanilla ice cream.

SERVES 4–6 (MAKES APPROX.
16 PANCAKES)
READY IN 30 MINUTES

225g self-raising flour
2 tsp baking powder
50g caster sugar
175ml buttermilk
2 medium eggs
175ml full-cream milk
500g Bramley apples
1 tsp vanilla extract
50g butter
Greek-style natural yogurt,
 to serve

For the toffee sauce:
50g unsalted butter
50g light muscovado sugar
2 tbsp golden syrup
2 tbsp double cream

1. Make the toffee sauce. Slowly bring the butter, sugar and golden syrup to the boil in a small pan, stirring, then simmer for 3 minutes until thick. Stir in the cream, then set aside to cool.

2. Sift the flour, baking powder and sugar into a bowl. Make a well in the centre, then add the buttermilk, eggs and milk. Whisk until smooth and thick. Peel, core and coarsely grate the apples and measure out 300g. Stir into the batter with the vanilla.

3. The pancakes should be cooked using clarified butter. To 'clarify' the butter, put it into a pan and leave over a low heat until melted. Remove from the heat and leave to stand for a few minutes. Then pour off the clear butter into a bowl and discard the milky-white solids at the bottom of the pan. Heat a large, non-stick frying pan over a medium heat. Brush the base with a little of the clarified butter, add 4 large spoonfuls of batter, spaced well apart, and cook for 2 minutes or until bubbles appear on top and they are golden underneath. Flip and cook for another minute. Transfer to a plate and keep warm while you cook the rest.

4. Pile the pancakes on to warmed plates, top with a large spoonful of yogurt and drizzle with the toffee sauce. Serve immediately.

★DELICIOUS. TIP Apples discolour quickly when peeled, so drop the pieces into lightly acidulated water (water and lemon juice) as you go.

Baked gooseberry, ginger and crème fraîche cheesecake

This rich, baked gooseberry cheesecake will keep in the fridge for up to 3 days.

SERVES 8–10

TAKES 1¼ HOURS, 1¼ HOURS BAKING, PLUS COOLING AND AT LEAST 4 HOURS CHILLING

Butter, for greasing
500g full-fat cream cheese
225g caster sugar
3 medium eggs
2 tbsp cornflour
5 tbsp ginger cordial
350g gooseberries, topped and tailed
200g tub crème fraîche

For the base:
100g ginger snap biscuits, crushed
100g digestive biscuits, crushed
2 tbsp demerara sugar
75g melted butter, warm

1. Preheat the oven to 150°C/fan 130°C/gas 2. Grease and base line a 23cm springform tin with baking paper. Make the base. Mix the biscuits and sugar into the melted butter, then press evenly into the base of the tin. Set aside.

2. Beat the cream cheese and 150g of the sugar in a bowl, then beat in the eggs, cornflour and 3 tablespoons of cordial. Pour into the tin and bake for 55 minutes, until set but slightly wobbly in the centre. Turn off the oven and leave to cool inside.

3. Meanwhile, simmer the gooseberries with 25g of sugar and the remaining cordial in a small pan for 5 minutes until just soft. Tip into a sieve set over a small pan and leave to drain. Then boil the juices until reduced to 2 tablespoons. Stir in the gooseberries and leave to cool.

4. Remove the cheesecake from the oven and re-set the temperature to 150°C/fan 130°C/gas 2. Mix the crème fraîche with the remaining 50g caster sugar. Spread the gooseberries over the cheesecake, then cover with the crème fraîche mixture. Bake for 15–20 minutes. Turn off the oven and leave to go cold inside. Cover and chill until the crème fraîche has set – at least 4 hours or overnight. Remove from the tin and serve in slices.

Variation This baked cheesecake is also very nice without gooseberries, flavoured with vanilla extract, lemon or orange zest instead of cordial and served with summer berries.

Individual summer puddings

These puddings are a real taste of summer with their mix of raspberries, blackcurrants and redcurrants.

MAKES 4

TAKES 30 MINUTES, PLUS COOLING
AND OVERNIGHT CHILLING

250g raspberries

125g blackcurrants, picked from the stalks

125g redcurrants, picked from the stalks

100g caster sugar

6 thin slices white bread, crusts removed

2 tbsp crème de cassis, plus extra to serve

1. Put the fruit and sugar in a pan over a medium heat. Gently simmer for 3–4 minutes, stirring occasionally, until the sugar has dissolved and the juices have begun to run from the fruit. Don't overcook the fruit: you want it to retain its shape and freshness. Remove from the heat and cool slightly.

2. Using a 6cm plain cutter, cut out 4 rounds from 2 slices of the bread (keep the trimmings). Dip both sides of the bread into the fruit, so the juices soak in, then use to line the base of 4 x 150ml individual pudding basins.

3. Tear the remaining bread into pieces and stir into the fruit mixture, along with the crème de cassis. Spoon into each mould and cover with cling film. Place on a baking sheet and weigh each one down – pots of yogurt are ideal. Chill overnight.

4. The next day, run a knife around each pudding to loosen, then turn out on to serving plates. Drizzle with extra crème de cassis to serve.

Berry pavlova squares with Cointreau strawberry coulis

Pavlovas are a seriously impressive dessert, and the meringue part is easier to make than you might think.

SERVES 8

TAKES 30 MINUTES, 45 MINUTES BAKING, PLUS COOLING AND CHILLING

Vegetable oil, for greasing
4 large egg whites
225g caster sugar
1 tbsp white wine vinegar
2 tsp cornflour
284ml carton double cream
1–2 tbsp Cointreau or similar orange liqueur, to taste
Fresh summer berries, to serve
Icing sugar, to dust

For the strawberry coulis:
225g strawberries, stalks removed
1 tbsp icing sugar
2 tbsp Cointreau or similar orange liqueur

1. Preheat the oven to 150°C/fan 130°C/gas 2. Lightly oil and line a 27cm x 17cm x 4cm deep rectangular tin with baking paper, making sure the paper is 3cm higher than the sides of the tin.

2. Whisk the egg whites in a large bowl to soft peaks. Whisk in the sugar, 1 tablespoon at a time, to form a thick meringue. Whisk in the vinegar and cornflour. Spoon evenly into the tin (it will be very full), and level the surface. Bake for 45 minutes, or until slightly risen and a very pale golden. Leave to cool completely in the tin.

3. Meanwhile, make the coulis. Whiz the strawberries, icing sugar and Cointreau in a food processor until smooth, then pass through a sieve into a bowl. Cover and chill.

4. Whisk the cream and Cointreau to soft peaks. Turn the pavlova out on to a board and trim away the edges with a large, wet, sharp knife. Spread over the cream. Cut into 8 squares and put on to plates. Top with some berries and dust with icing sugar. Drizzle the coulis around the plates and serve.

★ DELICIOUS. TIP You could make this pavlova the day before, then store in an airtight tin somewhere cool overnight – but don't decorate it in advance. The coulis will also keep overnight in the fridge.

Simple roasted rhubarb and lemon curd pots

The tangy rhubarb is a great match for the creamy mascarpone rippled with sweet lemon curd.

SERVES 4
TAKES 15 MINUTES, 15 MINUTES
BAKING, PLUS COOLING

400g forced rhubarb, cut
  into 4cm lengths
Small knob of butter
Grated zest and juice of 1 orange
75g golden caster sugar
380g jar good-quality
  lemon curd
250g tub mascarpone
4 stem ginger biscuits, crushed
Icing sugar, for dusting

1. Preheat the oven to 220°C/fan 200°C/gas 7. Scatter the rhubarb in 1 layer on a baking sheet. Dot with the butter, drizzle with the orange juice, sprinkle over the sugar and zest, and roast for 15 minutes until just tender. Set aside to cool.

2. Divide the rhubarb among 6 glasses or dishes. In a small bowl, roughly stir the lemon curd into the mascarpone with a kitchen knife to form a ripple effect and spoon on top of the rhubarb. Scatter over the biscuit crumbs and serve dusted with icing sugar.

Moist gooseberry, orange and almond dimple cake

So named because 'dimples' appear as the gooseberries sink into the moist cake during cooking. Serve warm with cream.

SERVES 8
TAKES 30 MINUTES, 45 MINUTES BAKING, PLUS COOLING

200g lightly salted butter, softened, plus extra to grease
100g self-raising flour
½ tsp baking powder
175g caster sugar, plus extra 2 tsp to decorate
Finely grated zest of 1 large orange
2 large eggs
100g ground almonds
175g red or green gooseberries, topped and tailed
25g light muscovado sugar
50g slivered almonds

1. Preheat the oven to 180°C/fan 160°C/gas 4. Grease and base line a 23cm springform tin with baking paper. Sift the flour with the baking powder into a bowl and set aside.

2. Beat 175g of the butter in a bowl until pale and creamy. Add the sugar and half the orange zest, and whisk until light and fluffy. Whisk in the eggs, one at a time, adding a spoonful of ground almonds with each egg. Gently stir in the remaining almonds and sifted flour.

3. Spoon the mixture into the tin and lightly level the surface. Bake for 20 minutes, then carefully slide the oven rack out and sprinkle the gooseberries evenly over the top. Bake for a further 10 minutes.

4. Meanwhile, melt the remaining butter, stir in the muscovado sugar, remaining orange zest and slivered almonds. Carefully remove the cake from the oven and scatter the almond mixture evenly over the top. Bake for a further 15 minutes, or until a skewer inserted into the centre comes out clean. Cool in the tin for 10 minutes, then remove and dust with a little more sugar.

Tangerine crêpes Suzette

Don't reserve these just for Pancake Day; enjoy these lacy pancakes in a lusciously boozy tangerine sauce any time of the year.

SERVES 4 (MAKES 8 CRÊPES)
READY IN 35 MINUTES

110g plain flour
1 tsp icing sugar
1 egg, lightly beaten
300ml milk
20g butter, melted, plus extra
  for cooking
Grated zest of 2 tangerines

For the sauce:
3 tbsp orange blossom honey
Juice of 5 tangerines
Juice of 1 small lemon
50g butter, cubed
4 tbsp Cointreau
2 tbsp brandy
Single cream or vanilla ice
  cream, to serve

1. Sift the flour, icing sugar and a pinch of salt into a bowl. Gradually whisk in the egg and milk until smooth. Stir in the melted butter and zest, and rest for 15 minutes.

2. Heat an 18cm non-stick frying pan over a medium heat. Melt a tiny knob of butter in the pan, add a ladleful of batter and swirl to create a thin pancake. Cook for 1–2 minutes until golden, then flip over and cook for 30 seconds. Set aside on a plate. Repeat to make 8 crêpes. Fold them into quarters.

3. For the sauce, cook the honey in a large, heavy-based pan over a medium heat for 3 minutes until it turns dark amber. Remove from the heat, add the fruit juices and cubed butter, and bring back to a simmer. Stir in the Cointreau.

4. Add the crêpes to the pan, spoon over the sauce and warm through. Take the pan to the table. Warm the brandy and light with a long match. Pour over the crêpes and serve with single cream or vanilla ice cream.

ice creams
and sorbets

Coconut and pineapple ice cream

Coconut and pineapple combine in this easy recipe to make the most delicious ice cream imaginable.

SERVES 4

TAKES 30 MINUTES, 20 MINUTES INFUSING, PLUS COOLING AND 3 HOURS FREEZING

400ml can coconut milk

Pared strip lime zest, plus juice of 1 lime

3 egg yolks

100g caster sugar

2 tsp cornflour

300g prepared pineapple chunks, plus extra wedges to serve

200ml double cream

Toasted coconut flakes, to serve

Pineapple leaves, to serve

1. Bring the coconut milk and lime zest almost to the boil in a pan, then remove from the heat and set aside to infuse for 20 minutes.

2. Whisk the egg yolks, sugar and cornflour together in a bowl until smooth. Gradually whisk in the coconut milk. Cook over a low heat, stirring, until the custard thickens. Remove from the heat and strain into a clean bowl. Discard the lime zest. Cover with baking paper and leave to cool.

3. Whiz the pineapple in a food processor into a rough purée. Stir into the custard with the cream and lime juice. Pour the mixture into a freezerproof container and freeze for 45 minutes. Remove, beat well, then return to the freezer for a further 2 hours. Alternatively, churn in an ice-cream maker until thick.

4. Serve scoops of ice cream with wedges of fresh pineapple. Sprinkle with toasted coconut and decorate with pineapple leaves, if you like.

★ DELICIOUS. TIP Buy a small fresh pineapple and slice into bite-sized pieces, or use canned pineapple chunks, drained of any syrup. If using fresh pineapple, reserve the green tops to decorate. Buy coconut flakes from health-food shops and lightly toast under a medium grill.

Caramel ice cream with chocolate peanut shards

This show-off caramel ice cream is enticing enough, but chocolate peanut shards make it something really sensational.

SERVES 6

TAKES 30 MINUTES, PLUS COOLING AND FREEZING

5 medium egg yolks
Seeds of 1 vanilla pod
125g caster sugar
284ml carton double cream
225ml full-fat milk
150g plain chocolate, broken into pieces
50g natural roasted peanuts (from health-food shops), roughly chopped
½ tsp sea salt

1. Whisk the egg yolks and vanilla seeds together in a bowl for 3–4 minutes, until pale and thick.

2. Dissolve the sugar and 3 tablespoons of water in a pan over a low heat, then boil until the mixture forms a golden caramel. Remove from the heat and add the cream – be careful, it will spit! Add the milk and heat gently to re-melt the caramel.

3. Stir the caramel mixture into the egg yolks. Return to the pan and stir over a medium–low heat until it coats the back of the spoon. Cool, then strain into a freezerproof container, cover and freeze until firm. Whiz in a food processor until smooth, return to the container and re-freeze. Repeat twice more, then freeze until hard. Alternatively, churn in an ice-cream maker.

4. To serve, melt the chocolate and spread it out thinly on to a large board lined with baking paper. Sprinkle over and lightly press in the nuts. Sprinkle with the salt and chill until hardened. Cut into long, jagged shards and serve with the ice cream.

Strawberry and mascarpone gelato slabs

A classic combination, and one of the easiest and most delicious ice creams you could possibly make.

SERVES 6

TAKES 30 MINUTES, ABOUT 1 HOUR MACERATING, PLUS OVERNIGHT FREEZING

300g strawberries, hulled and chopped

2 tbsp elderflower cordial

150g golden caster sugar

500g mascarpone

100g white chocolate, roughly chopped

For the soft strawberries:

200g strawberries, hulled and quartered

1 tbsp elderflower cordial

2 tbsp golden caster sugar

1. Put the chopped strawberries in a bowl. Add the cordial and sprinkle over the sugar. Set aside to macerate for up to 1 hour.

2. Beat the mascarpone and white chocolate together, then fold through the strawberry mixture. Put it in a cling-film-lined, straight-sided freezerproof box (about 1 litre) and freeze it overnight.

3. For the soft strawberries, put the berries and cordial in a bowl, then sprinkle with sugar. Set aside for 15 minutes. Slice the ice cream and spoon over the strawberries to serve.

Variation Try swapping the elderflower cordial for a blackcurrant-flavoured one. It goes incredibly well with the white chocolate.

Lemon curd and poppy seed ice cream loaf

This lovely ice cream is a delightfully simple way to finish off any meal.

SERVES 10
TAKES 20 MINUTES, PLUS OVERNIGHT FREEZING

2 tbsp poppy seeds
4 medium egg yolks
1 medium egg
150g golden caster sugar
Finely grated zest of 1 lemon
284ml carton double cream, lightly whipped until just thickened
300g jar good-quality lemon curd

1. Brush a 900g loaf tin with water, then line with cling film, leaving the excess overhanging.

2. Lightly bruise the poppy seeds using a pestle and mortar. Set aside.

3. Put the egg yolks, whole egg, sugar and lemon zest into a large, heatproof bowl. Rest over a pan of just simmering water and whisk, using an electric hand whisk, for 5 minutes, until very thick and pale. Remove the bowl from the pan and whisk for another 5 minutes, until cool.

4. Fold the cooled mixture into the whipped cream, along with the poppy seeds. Briefly mix in the lemon curd, so it looks slightly streaky. Tip into the prepared tin, level the surface and cover with the cling film. Freeze overnight.

5. To serve, dip the base of the tin briefly in hot water, then turn out on to a serving plate. Remove the cling film and leave at room temperature for 5 minutes. Cut into slices and serve with dessert biscuits.

Variation Other curds would also work well in this dessert, such as lime or orange. Try to echo the flavour by swapping the zest for lime or orange too.

Orange ice cream with caramel and cardamom brittle

The flavours of orange and cardamom are a refreshing combination in this glamorous ice cream.

SERVES 6

TAKES 1 HOUR, PLUS COOLING AND FREEZING

4 large oranges
500ml single cream
125g golden caster sugar
500ml ready-made custard
  (or home-made, see page 185)
2 tbsp Cointreau or similar
  orange liqueur

For the caramel and cardamom brittle:

125g caster sugar
Pinch of roughly crushed
  cardamom seeds

1. Finely grate the zest from the oranges and put three-quarters of it into a pan with the cream and sugar. Heat very gently for 30 minutes. Transfer to a bowl and leave to cool.

2. Juice 3 of the oranges into a small pan and simmer until reduced by half. Cool completely. Segment the remaining orange.

3. Purée the segments and remaining zest, then stir into the custard with the Cointreau. Strain over cream mixture, discarding the zest and stir in with the orange juice. Churn in an ice-cream maker, or pour the mixture into a freezerproof container and freeze for 3 hours or until almost solid, then whiz in a food processor until smooth, then re-freeze. Repeat twice more, then freeze until firm.

4. To make the brittle, line a baking sheet with foil. Put the sugar in a pan with 5 tablespoons of boiling water, and when dissolved add the cardamom and boil rapidly until it turns a pale caramel colour. Pour on to a foil-lined baking sheet and when cold, break into shards. Use to decorate the ice cream.

Variation Don't really fancy cardamom? Then leave it out and add a few lightly toasted flaked almonds to the caramel just before you pour it out.

Rhubarb and buttermilk ice cream with rhubarb compote

This stunning dessert is beautiful to look at and divine to eat: the ice cream is perfectly complemented by the sharp rhubarb.

SERVES 6
TAKES 20 MINUTES, PLUS FREEZING

150g caster sugar
Zest of ½ lemon
½ vanilla pod, split lengthways
500ml double cream
500ml buttermilk

For the rhubarb compote:
Juice of 2 oranges
2 tbsp caster sugar
1 vanilla pod, split lengthways
1kg forced rhubarb, trimmed, washed and cut into 2cm chunks

1. Make the compote. Put the orange juice, sugar and vanilla in a pan over a low heat, and stir until the sugar dissolves. Add the rhubarb and bring to a simmer, then remove from the heat. Cover and set aside for 10 minutes. The rhubarb pieces should break down into a compote in that time. If not, cover for another 5 minutes, then remove the vanilla pod. Chill for up to 3–4 days.

2. Make the ice cream. Put the sugar, lemon zest and vanilla together in a pan. Add the cream and bring to a very gentle simmer on the hob, stirring, until the sugar dissolves. Cool completely, strain into a bowl and stir in the buttermilk.

3. Churn in an ice-cream maker, or pour the mixture into a freezer-proof container and freeze for 3 hours or until almost solid. Whiz in a food processor until smooth, then re-freeze. Repeat twice more, then return to the freezer until needed. Serve scoops of ice cream with the compote.

★ DELICIOUS. TIP Forced rhubarb is always beautifully pink, and that is what makes this dessert so attractive.

Lemon and lime granita

This frozen Italian dessert has the tangy flavour of fresh lemons and limes – and hardly any calories!

SERVES 4
TAKES 20 MINUTES, PLUS COOLING
AND FREEZING

2 large juicy lemons
2 juicy limes
100g caster sugar

1. Peel the zest from the lemons and limes using a potato peeler and chop roughly. Put the sugar, 150ml of water and the zest into a pan, and stir over a gentle heat, until the mixture comes to a simmer and the sugar dissolves. Remove from the heat and cool.

2. Squeeze the juice from the lemons and limes and stir into the sugar syrup. Strain the mixture into a shallow freezerproof container with a lid, cover, and freeze until the mixture begins to freeze at the edges – about 2 hours.

3. Scrape all the ice from the sides of the box and break up into smaller crystals with a fork. Re-cover and return to the freezer. Repeat every 30 minutes, until you have a frozen but grainy mixture. Return to the freezer until you are ready to serve.

4. Spoon into tall glass tumblers, decorate with a twist of lemon or lime zest, if you like, and serve.

Hazelnut meringue and chocolate ice cream

Buying good ingredients makes this indulgent ice cream even more of a treat.

SERVES 6–8

TAKES 30 MINUTES, PLUS 45 MINUTES IN THE OVEN (FOR THE MERINGUES), PLUS COOLING AND FREEZING

100g caster sugar

4 tbsp unsweetened cocoa powder

1 tsp cornflour

3 egg yolks

375ml full-fat milk

150g Green & Black's Organic Maya Gold dark chocolate, finely chopped

284ml carton whipping cream

For the hazelnut meringues:

3 egg whites

200g caster sugar

50g hazelnuts, toasted and chopped

1. For the meringues, preheat the oven to 120°C/fan 100°C/gas ½. Whisk the egg whites until stiff, then gradually whisk in the sugar to form a stiff meringue. Fold in the hazelnuts. Drop 18 spoonfuls on to 2 lined baking sheets and bake for 30 minutes. Increase the oven temperature to 140°C/fan 120°C/gas 1 and bake for another 15 minutes. Cool.

2. Dissolve the sugar in 100ml of water in a small pan over a low heat. Boil for 1 minute, then tip into a bowl and cool. Add the cocoa, cornflour and egg yolks, and whisk until smooth. Boil the milk in a large pan and gradually stir in. Return to the pan, and cook gently for 5 minutes, stirring, until it coats the back of the spoon. Stir in the chocolate until melted. Cool. In a bowl, lightly whip the cream and fold into the chocolate mix.

3. Churn in an ice-cream maker, or pour into a freezerproof container and freeze until almost solid. Whiz in a food processor until smooth, then re-freeze. Repeat twice more. Roughly break up 4 meringues and fold in. Return to the freezer until frozen hard.

4. Soften in the fridge for 10 minutes before serving. Crumble the remaining meringues and serve scattered on top.

Espresso granita

This chic espresso granita is low in calories, virtually fat-free and a coffee-lover's dream.

SERVES 6

TAKES 15 MINUTES, PLUS COOLING AND FREEZING

150g caster sugar

4 tbsp good-quality ground coffee

Pared zest of 1 orange

Whipped cream, to serve (optional)

1. Put the sugar and 150ml of water in a small pan over a low heat. Leave to dissolve, then increase the heat and boil for 1 minute. Cool.

2. Bring the coffee, 500ml of water and the orange zest to the boil in a pan and boil for 1 minute. Remove from the heat and set aside until cold.

3. Strain the coffee mixture through a muslin-lined sieve into a shallow freezerproof container. Mix in the sugar syrup, cover, and freeze for 2 hours. Scrape all the ice from the sides of the box and break up into smaller crystals with a fork. Re-cover and return to the freezer. Repeat every 30 minutes, until you have a frozen but grainy mixture. Return to the freezer until you are ready to serve.

4. To serve, separate the grains with a fork and spoon into glasses. Top with a dollop of whipped cream, if you like.

Pear sorbet with pear wafers

Get a double dose of the popular fruit in this surprisingly healthy recipe.

SERVES 6–8

TAKES 45 MINUTES, PLUS 2 HOURS IN THE OVEN (FOR THE WAFERS), PLUS FREEZING

1kg firm ripe dessert pears, such as Comice
100g caster sugar
Juice of 1 lemon
4 tbsp pear liqueur (Poire William) or calvados

For the pear wafers:
75g caster sugar
2 dessert pears

1. Make the sorbet. Peel, core and slice the pears into a pan, and add the sugar and 100ml of water. Simmer for 15 minutes, until the pears are soft. Cool, then whiz in a blender with the lemon juice until smooth. Stir in the liqueur.

2. Churn in an ice-cream maker, or pour into a freezerproof container and freeze for 2 hours. Break up the ice crystals with a fork and re-freeze. Transfer to a food processor and whiz until smooth. Return to the freezer until needed.

3. Meanwhile, make the pear wafers. Preheat the oven to 110°C/fan 90°C/gas ¼. Dissolve the sugar in 50ml of water in a pan over a low heat, then boil for 2–3 minutes. Cool.

4. Slice the pears very thinly. Discard any smaller slices. Coat them in the syrup, lay on a lined baking sheet and bake for 2 hours, turning halfway, until dried and crisp. Loosen from the paper, then leave to cool.

5. Soften the sorbet in the fridge for 10 minutes before serving. Scoop into bowls and decorate with a pear wafer.

Limoncello semifreddo with strawberries

Limoncello is a lemon-flavoured liqueur from Italy and combines well with strawberries in this quick and easy recipe.

SERVES 8

TAKES 10 MINUTES, PLUS FREEZING AND CHILLING

4 large very fresh eggs
75g caster sugar
500ml double cream
150ml limoncello, plus extra 4 tbsp
1kg small strawberries, hulled and halved
Finely grated zest of 1 large lemon and 2½ tbsp fresh lemon juice
4 tbsp icing sugar

1. Separate the eggs into 2 large mixing bowls. Add the sugar to the egg yolks and beat for a few minutes with an electric hand whisk until pale and thick.

2. In another bowl, whip the cream to soft peaks. Using clean beaters, whisk the egg whites to stiff, but not dry, peaks.

3. Fold the cream into the egg yolks, then fold in the 150ml of limoncello. Carefully fold in the egg whites. Spoon the mixture into a shallow 2.5-litre serving dish, about 5cm deep, cover with cling film and put in the freezer until needed – at least 7–8 hours.

4. About 20 minutes before serving, put the strawberries into a bowl. Add the lemon zest, lemon juice, the icing sugar and the extra 4 tablespoons of limoncello. Gently stir together, cover and chill for 20 minutes.

5. To serve, scoop large spoonfuls of the semifreddo on to dessert plates and spoon some of the strawberries alongside. Serve immediately as semifreddo melts faster than normal ice cream.

Note: This recipe contains raw egg.

Amaretti tortoni with brandy snaps and raspberries

These simple, individual ice creams can be made well ahead of time, making them ideal for entertaining.

SERVES 6–8

TAKES 30 MINUTES, 8 HOURS FREEZING, PLUS COOLING

142ml carton single cream
284ml carton double cream
2 egg whites
3 tbsp dark rum or sweet sherry
30g caster sugar
75g amaretti biscuits or
  macaroons, coarsely crushed
Brandy snaps, raspberries and
  icing sugar, to serve

1. Put both creams and the egg whites into a large bowl and whisk vigorously using an electric hand whisk for about 8 minutes, until the mixture forms soft peaks. Whisk in the rum or sherry, then gradually whisk in the sugar. Gently fold in the crushed biscuits.

2. Divide the mixture among six individual soufflé dishes (8cm diameter x 5.5cm deep) or 225ml ramekins. Cover with cling film and freeze for 8 hours until firm, or for up to 1 month.

3. To serve, remove the tortoni from the freezer and leave them to soften very slightly at room temperature for 15 minutes. Dip each dish briefly in hot water, then turn out on to plates. Arrange the brandy snaps and raspberries alongside. Dust with icing sugar and serve.

Note: This recipe contains raw egg.

★ DELICIOUS. TIP If you don't have individual moulds, freeze the tortoni in a 1-litre loaf tin, then slice to serve. Serve any leftover brandy snaps with coffee after a meal on another day.

Malai kulfi (Indian almond and pistachio ice cream)

The evaporated and condensed milks make this ice cream so different, giving it a unique, rich and creamy flavour.

SERVES 8
TAKES 25 MINUTES, PLUS
6–8 HOURS FREEZING

397g can condensed milk
410g can evaporated milk
300ml whipping cream
¼ tsp freshly ground cardamom
  seeds (not pods)
Few drops of vanilla essence
25g ground almonds
25g ground pistachio nuts,
  plus extra whole nuts
  to garnish
Fresh mint leaves, to garnish

1. Put the condensed milk, evaporated milk and cream in a large pan, and bring to the boil. Simmer for 15 minutes, stirring constantly until slightly reduced and thickened. Stir in the cardamom and vanilla essence, then remove from the heat and leave to cool completely.

2. Mix in the ground almonds and pistachio nuts and pour into 8 x 100ml dariole moulds or empty yogurt pots. Freeze for 6–8 hours, or until firm.

3. To serve, dip the moulds briefly in warm water and turn out on to plates. Decorate with the whole pistachios and mint, and serve.

Variation To make this even more special, try serving it with a finely diced fruit salad of fresh mango and pineapple, dressed with a little passion fruit pulp.

Raspberry and redcurrant sorbet

Capture the flavour of ruby-red summer berries with this delicious sorbet. Serve casually in cones, or in glasses with a little prosecco poured over it.

SERVES 4–6
TAKES 20 MINUTES, PLUS FREEZING

185g caster sugar
375g raspberries
125g redcurrants, stalks removed
Juice of 1 lemon

1. Put the sugar and 185ml of water in a small pan over a low heat. Stir to dissolve the sugar, then increase the heat and boil for 1 minute, until syrupy. Set aside to cool.

2. Put the fruit, lemon juice and cooled sugar syrup in a blender or liquidiser, and whiz to a purée. Rest a sieve over a large bowl and press the berry purée through it, using the back of a ladle. Discard the pips that remain in the sieve.

3. Churn in an ice-cream maker, or pour into a freezerproof container and freeze for 2 hours. Break up the ice crystals with a fork and re-freeze. Then transfer to a processor and whiz until smooth. Return to the freezer until needed.

4. To serve, transfer the sorbet to the fridge for about 10 minutes, or until scoopable. Serve in waffle ice-cream cones or dessert bowls.

creamy
desserts and
mousses

Blueberry syllabub trifles

Trifles made in individual glasses always look much smarter than those served up from one large bowl – which makes them great for entertaining.

SERVES 6
TAKES 25 MINUTES, PLUS COOLING
AND CHILLING

200g good Madeira cake, lemon
  or plain sponge, cut into cubes
4 tbsp amaretto
125g golden caster sugar
Juice and finely grated zest of
  1 lemon
300g blueberries
5 tbsp sweet dessert wine
284ml carton double cream
Flaked almonds, toasted,
  to serve

1. Divide the cake among 6 x 250ml glasses or put into a 1.5-litre bowl. Drizzle with the amaretto and set aside.

2. Put 100g of the sugar, the lemon juice and 1 tablespoon of water into a pan over a medium heat. Bring to a simmer and cook for 5 minutes. Stir in half the blueberries and simmer for 2–3 minutes to soften the fruit. Cool slightly, then whiz in a food processor until smooth. Tip into a bowl and stir in most of the remaining whole blueberries. Cool completely, then spoon over the sponge layer.

3. Make the syllabub. Put the wine, remaining sugar and the lemon zest into a small pan. Simmer for 3–4 minutes until reduced slightly. Cool completely.

4. Pour the cream into a large bowl and gradually whisk in the wine to soft peaks. Spoon on top of the blueberries. Chill until ready to serve, or overnight. Decorate with the remaining blueberries and the almonds.

Variation These would also be very nice made with raspberries. There's no need to cook them first: just purée half with some sugar to taste, then stir in the remainder.

Summer fruit Eton Mess

Though it looks like this dessert takes a long time to make, there's next-to-no work involved.

SERVES 6
TAKES 2 HOURS

150g raspberries
150g blueberries
250g strawberries, hulled and roughly chopped
4 tbsp crème de cassis
500g Greek yogurt
1 fresh mint sprig

For the meringues:
3 large free-range egg whites
175g caster sugar
½ tsp vanilla extract

1. Preheat the oven to 140°C/fan 120°C/gas 1. Make the meringues. Whisk the egg whites in a large, clean bowl to soft peaks. Whisk in the sugar, 1 tablespoon at a time, to make a stiff and glossy meringue. Whisk in the vanilla extract.

2. Line a large baking sheet with baking paper. Using a large metal spoon, drop craggy dollops of meringue on to the paper, well spaced apart. Bake for 1½ hours. Lift off the paper and cool on a wire rack.

3. Put the fruit into a bowl with the crème de cassis, gently toss together and set aside for 15 minutes, until juicy. Put the yogurt in a large bowl and lightly fold in three-quarters of the berries, leaving the juice behind. Roughly crumble in three of the meringues and briefly mix. Spoon into six glasses, top with the remaining juicy berries and garnish each with a fresh mint sprig to serve.

★ DELICIOUS. TIP This recipe will make more meringues than you need, but they will keep in an airtight container for up to 1 week. If you don't have time to make meringues, just buy some ready-made.

Variation Eton Mess is traditionally made with whipped cream, so replace half or even all the yogurt with some lightly whipped double cream, if you wish.

Creamy lemon blancmange

Rum gives this mouthwatering lemon dessert an extra kick
– and the edible flowers show it off to best effect.

SERVES 6
TAKES 20 MINUTES, PLUS COOLING,
SETTING AND 4 HOURS OR OVERNIGHT
CHILLING

5 strips pared lemon zest
450ml full-fat milk
40g caster sugar
40g ground almonds
5 sheets of leaf gelatine
340ml double cream
5 tbsp white rum
Edible flowers, to serve

1. Put the lemon zest, milk, sugar and ground almonds into a pan, and bring to the boil. Reduce the heat and simmer for 10 minutes, stirring occasionally. Set aside to cool slightly.

2. Meanwhile, place the leaf gelatine in a shallow dish, pour cold water over them and it to soak for about 5 minutes, until soft. Lift the leaves out of the water, squeeze out the excess and stir into the hot milk until completely melted. Stir in the cream and white rum.

3. Pour the mixture into 6 x 150ml individual jelly moulds and set aside to cool. Cover with cling film, transfer to the fridge and allow to set and chill for at least 4 hours, or overnight.

4. When ready to serve, bring back to room temperature. Then dip the moulds very briefly in hot water to loosen. Turn out on to plates and serve decorated with edible flowers, such as pansies and nasturtiums.

Variation Not a fan of rum? Then replace it with 5 tablespoons of an orange-flavoured liqueur, such as Cointreau, instead.

White chocolate and blueberry jelly creams

We don't tend to make jellies any more, but the luscious flavour combination in this recipe will bring them back into style.

SERVES 6

TAKES 25 MINUTES, PLUS COOLING, SETTING AND 4 HOURS OR OVERNIGHT CHILLING

3 sheets of gelatine
75ml mixed berry fruit cordial
150g blueberries
125g good-quality white chocolate, broken into pieces
284ml carton double cream

1. Cover two of the leaf gelatine sheets with cold water and leave to soak for 5 minutes, until soft. Mix the cordial with 300ml of hot water from the kettle. Lift the leaf gelatine out of the water and whisk into the cordial until completely melted. Divide the mixture equally among the bases of 6 x 120ml individual moulds or ramekins. Divide the blueberries among each mould. Leave to cool, then chill for 1 hour or until completely set.

2. Meanwhile, soak the remaining leaf gelatine in cold water as before. Place the white chocolate and cream in a bowl set over a pan of barely simmering water and leave until melted. Remove the bowl from the pan and stir until smooth. Add the leaf gelatine and whisk until melted. Leave to cool completely. Spoon into the moulds and chill for a further 4 hours or overnight until set.

3. To serve, dip the moulds briefly in hot water to loosen, then turn out on to serving plates.

Lemon curd and ginger fool

A lusciously creamy dessert that's ready in a jiffy.

SERVES 6
READY IN 10 MINUTES

1 ball stem ginger in syrup,
  finely chopped, plus 1 tbsp
  syrup
75g mascarpone
4 tbsp icing sugar
250ml double cream
8 tbsp good-quality lemon curd
Ginger thin biscuits, to serve
  (optional)

1. Beat the stem ginger syrup, mascarpone and icing sugar together in a large bowl until smooth.

2. Put the cream into another bowl and whisk until it forms soft peaks. Lightly fold into the mascarpone mixture, then stir through the lemon curd with a fork so it is streaked.

3. Divide the lemon curd fool among six glasses and top with the chopped stem ginger. Serve with ginger thin biscuits, if you like.

Baileys cream with strawberries in syrup

These are like crème brûlée flavoured with Baileys, but the strawberries in syrup give it a unique taste.

SERVES 6
TAKES ABOUT 1 HOUR, PLUS COOLING AND CHILLING

8 egg yolks
100g caster sugar
500ml double cream
100ml Baileys

For the strawberries in syrup:
900g small strawberries,
  hulls removed
1 tbsp caster sugar
Seeds of 1 vanilla pod

1. Preheat the oven to 150°C/fan 130°C/gas 2. Lightly mix the egg yolks and sugar together in a bowl.

2. Bring the cream and Baileys to the boil in a pan, briefly mix into the egg yolks, then strain into a large jug.

3. Divide among 6 x 150ml heatproof teacups or ramekins. Put into a roasting tin and pour in hot (not boiling) water to come halfway up the sides of the dishes. Cover the tin with foil and bake for 25–30 minutes, until the custards are set but still slightly wobbly. Remove from the tin, cool, then chill.

4. Meanwhile, make the strawberries in syrup. Thickly slice half the strawberries and put into a heatproof bowl with the sugar and vanilla seeds. Cover with cling film, rest over a pan of simmering water and leave for 30 minutes, to draw out the juices. Leave to cool, then chill.

5. Tip the strawberries into a sieve set over a bowl and leave to drain. Discard the berries. Stir the remaining strawberries into the syrup, spoon on to the custards, and serve.

Gooseberry and elderflower fool

This is one of the nicest, yet most simple ways in which to make the most of gooseberries and elderflowers during the few weeks in June and July that they are around.

SERVES 4
TAKES 25 MINUTES, PLUS COOLING
AND AT LEAST 1 HOUR CHILLING

500g gooseberries
100g caster sugar
2 strips pared lemon zest
2 elderflower heads (optional)
3 tbsp elderflower cordial, or
  to taste
142ml carton double cream
150ml fresh ready-made vanilla
  custard
Sponge finger biscuits, to serve

1. Put the gooseberries into a pan (there is no need to top and tail them) with 2 tablespoons of the sugar, the lemon zest, and the elderflower heads, if using. Cook over a low heat until the juices start to run from the gooseberries, then cover and cook for 5 minutes or until the berries are soft. Remove and discard the elderflower heads and add the remaining sugar. Increase the heat slightly and cook for 4–5 minutes to reduce the liquid slightly. Leave to go cold.

2. Remove and discard the lemon zest from the pan. Rub the fruit through a sieve into a bowl and stir in the elderflower cordial, to taste.

3. In another bowl, whip the cream until it just starts to form soft peaks. Carefully fold the custard into the purée, followed by the cream, so that the mixture is nicely marbled. Spoon into four serving glasses and chill for at least 1 hour before serving. Serve with sponge fingers.

★ DELICIOUS. TIP It is important that the gooseberry purée, custard and whipped cream are all of the same consistency, so that they combine nicely into a soft, green cloud.

Coffee and rum tiramisu with molasses topping

What makes this tiramisu different is the topping: the molasses sugar turns into a rich caramel sauce.

SERVES 6–8
TAKES 20 MINUTES, PLUS 2 HOURS CHILLING

150ml freshly made espresso coffee, or 4 tsp instant coffee dissolved in 150ml boiling water
4 tbsp dark rum
5 tsp molasses sugar
40g golden caster sugar
2 medium eggs, separated
250g tub mascarpone
Few drops of vanilla extract
20 Savoiardi or sponge finger biscuits
1 tbsp dark muscovado sugar

1. Mix together the coffee, rum and 2 teaspoons of the molasses sugar. Pour into a small, shallow dish.

2. Set aside 2 tablespoons of the caster sugar. Beat the egg yolks and the remaining caster sugar together in a bowl for 4 minutes until pale and thick.

3. Beat the mascarpone cheese in another bowl until smooth, then mix into the egg-yolk mixture with the vanilla extract. Whisk the egg whites in a bowl to soft peaks. Gradually whisk in the reserved caster sugar to form a soft meringue. Gently fold into the mascarpone mixture.

4. Briefly dip half the sponge fingers, one at a time, into the coffee mixture and lay them side by side on a serving plate or dish. Evenly spoon over half of the mascarpone mixture. Repeat once more. Chill for 1½ hours.

5. Mix the remaining molasses sugar with the dark muscovado sugar to remove any lumps. Sprinkle over the top of the dessert and chill for another 15–20 minutes before serving.

Note: This recipe contains raw egg.

Peach zabaglione

This light, summery recipe requires a little elbow grease but is
well worth the extra effort.

4–5 ripe peaches

**75g caster sugar, plus extra
1–2 tbsp to taste**

**175ml Marsala, Vin Santo or
amontillado sherry, plus extra
3 tbsp**

6 large egg yolks

1. Halve the peaches, remove the stones, then
carefully pull off the skins. Slice into a large frying
pan over a medium–high heat and sprinkle with
the extra sugar to taste, and the Marsala, Vin Santo
or sherry. Fry briskly for 2–3 minutes, until just
tender. Spoon into 6 dessert glasses and set aside.

2. Put the egg yolks and 75g of sugar into a
stainless-steel or heatproof glass bowl, and whisk
with an electric hand whisk for 5 minutes, until
thick and pale yellow.

3. Place the bowl over a pan of barely simmering
water and whisk for another 15 minutes, drizzling
in a little of the remaining Marsala, Vin Santo or
sherry every now and then, until the mixture
almost triples in volume and is light, foamy and
holding in soft peaks. Take care not to get the
mixture too hot or it will start to cook. Spoon on
top of the peaches and serve while still warm.

Chestnut and almond creams

Chestnuts have a wonderfully distinctive flavour, so try using them in their puréed form to make this yummy dessert.

SERVES 4
TAKES 25 MINUTES, PLUS
6–7 MINUTES IN THE OVEN,
PLUS COOLING

25g whole blanched almonds
225g canned chestnut purée
100g caster sugar
200ml crème fraîche
Runny honey (chestnut if
  possible), to drizzle

1. Cover the blanched almonds with boiling water and soak for 10 minutes. Drain and slice lengthways into thin shards. Preheat the oven to 200°C/fan 180°C/gas 6. Spread the nuts out on a baking sheet and roast for 6–7 minutes, until golden. Remove and leave to cool.

2. Put the chestnut purée in a small pan over a gentle heat and warm through – don't let it get too hot. Beat in the sugar (the purée will go glossy and dark). Transfer to a bowl and leave to cool.

3. Drop alternate teaspoonfuls of the chestnut purée and crème fraîche into 4 x 150ml dessert glasses and swirl with the handle of a spoon. Drizzle with a little honey and scatter with the almonds to serve.

Mojito cheesecakes

These have all the flavours of the classic cocktail: rum, lime, sugar and mint. Deliciously creamy, yet sharp and light at the same time.

SERVES 6
TAKES 20 MINUTES, PLUS AT LEAST 1 HOUR CHILLING

25g butter
150g thin almond biscuits, crushed
4 limes
100g light muscovado sugar
4 tbsp rum
Large handful of fresh mint leaves, plus extra sprigs to decorate
400g cottage cheese
250g tub mascarpone
150ml whipping cream

1. Melt the butter in a pan, then stir in the biscuits until combined. Divide among six glasses and press down well. Chill.

2. Finely grate the zest and squeeze the juice from 3 limes. In a small pan, dissolve the sugar in 5 tablespoons of water, then bring to the boil and simmer for 2 minutes without stirring. Remove from the heat and stir in the lime zest, lime juice, rum and mint. Leave to cool.

3. Put the cottage cheese and mascarpone into a food processor and whiz briefly until smooth. Strain over the lime and mint syrup and beat briefly until smooth and creamy. Spoon on to the biscuit bases and chill for at least 1 hour.

4. When ready to serve, beat the cream until thick. Spoon a little on to each cheesecake. Slice the remaining lime into thin rounds and use to decorate the tops, along with the mint sprigs.

Strawberry shrikhand (Indian spiced yogurt)

This is one of the easiest desserts in the world to make and the ideal way to finish off any spicy meal.

SERVES 6
TAKES 10 MINUTES, PLUS DRAINING

500g Greek yogurt
200g strawberries, hulled
Icing sugar, to taste
¼–½ tsp freshly ground
  cardamom seeds (not pods)
Freshly hulled strawberries,
  quartered, to decorate
Blanched pistachio nuts, roughly
  chopped, to decorate

1. Tip the yogurt into a fine sieve set over a bowl, and leave to strain in the fridge for about 1 hour.

2. Put the 200g of strawberries into a food processor and whiz briefly to make a smooth sauce. Sweeten to taste with some icing sugar.

3. Tip the strained yogurt into a bowl and stir in the cardamom and a little icing sugar to taste. Quickly stir the strawberry sauce through the yogurt, so that it remains streaky, and divide among six individual glass bowls. Cover and chill until required.

4. Just before serving, sprinkling the top of the yogurts with the quartered strawberries and pistachios.

Burnt creams with mango, lime and five spice

Mango and five spice make a brilliant partnership here, and the flavours are zinged up by the lime and mellowed by a brûlée topping.

MAKES 6
TAKES 35 MINUTES, 30–35 MINUTES BAKING, PLUS COOLING AND 4 HOURS OR OVERNIGHT CHILLING

1kg (4 medium) ripe mangoes, peeled and cut into 1.5cm dice
Grated zest of 1 lime, plus juice of 2 small limes
75g soft brown sugar
1¼ tsp five spice powder
500ml whipping cream
4 medium egg yolks
75g caster sugar
2 tsp ground ginger

1. Put the mango, lime zest, lime juice, brown sugar and five spice into a small stainless-steel pan. Simmer, stirring, for 8–10 minutes until soft. Remove from the heat, mash half the mango, then stir together.

2. Preheat the oven to 160°C/ fan 140°C/gas 3. Heat the cream in a pan. Mix the yolks in a bowl with 25g of the caster sugar. Stir in the cream, return to the pan and stir over a low heat for 5 minutes until the custard lightly coats the back of the spoon.

3. Divide the mango among 6 x 150ml ramekins. Strain over the custard, being careful not to mix the two. Place in a roasting tin and pour in hot water to come 2–3cm up the sides of the ramekins. Bake for 30–35 minutes, until just set. Cool, then chill for at least 4 hours, or overnight.

4. Preheat the grill to its highest setting. Mix the remaining caster sugar with the ginger and sprinkle over the custards. Clean off any sugar from the rims of the dishes, then place in a roasting tin containing 2cm of iced water. Grill for 1–2 minutes until the sugar has caramelised. Serve immediately.

★ DELICIOUS. TIP This dessert is heavenly served ice-cold at the bottom and hot and caramelised on top. Therefore, they are best made the day before and grilled just before serving.

Vanilla tart with poached apricots

This is a beautiful, creamy tart, delicately flavoured with
vanilla, which is a perfect match with the poached apricots.

SERVES 8

TAKES 50 MINUTES, ABOUT 1 HOUR
BAKING, PLUS CHILLING AND COOLING

350g sweet shortcrust pastry
  (shop-bought or for
  homemade, see page 183)
568ml carton double cream
1 vanilla pod, split lengthways
3 eggs, plus 1 egg yolk
75g caster sugar
Icing sugar, for dusting

For the poached apricots:

115g caster sugar
1 vanilla pod, split lengthways
  and seeds scraped
12 fresh apricots, halved and
  stoned

1. Make a 25cm pastry case that is 2cm deep with
the pastry and bake it blind (see page 184).

2. Lower the oven temperature to 150°C/
fan 130°C/gas 2. For the filling, bring the cream
and vanilla pod to the boil in a pan. Leave to cool,
then scrape the seeds from the pod into the cream.
Discard the pod.

3. Beat the eggs, egg yolk, sugar and cream
together. Pour into the pastry case and bake for
30–35 minutes, until very softly set. Leave to
cool completely.

4. Meanwhile, make the poached apricots. Warm
the sugar, vanilla pod and seeds and 750ml of
water in a wide pan until the sugar has dissolved.
Add the apricots and simmer for 5 minutes, until
tender. Remove with a slotted spoon to a bowl. Boil
the remaining syrup until reduced by half. Pour
over the apricots and leave to cool completely.

5. Dust the tart with icing sugar and serve with the
poached apricots.

Glazed pear and macadamia tart

The flavour of both the pears and vanilla go well with the sweetness of the caramel in this delightfully sticky tart.

SERVES 8
TAKES 45 MINUTES, 35–40 MINUTES BAKING, PLUS CHILLING AND COOLING

1kg firm, just-ripe pears
55g salted butter
65g caster sugar
1 tsp freshly ground star anise
1 vanilla pod, split lengthways
1 tbsp fresh lemon juice
2 tbsp Poire William liqueur
350g sweet shortcrust pastry
  (shop-bought or for
  homemade, see page 183)
1 egg white, for brushing
50g macadamia nuts, chopped
Vanilla ice cream, to serve

1. Peel, quarter and core the pears, then cut into 1cm wedges. Simmer in a wide, stainless-steel pan with the butter, sugar, star anise, vanilla pod and lemon juice for 15–20 minutes, until just tender. Stir in the Poire William and leave to cool.

2. Preheat the oven to 180°C/ fan 160°C/gas 4 and put in a baking sheet to heat up. Thinly roll out the pastry and use to line a 25cm round, 2cm deep loose-bottomed tart tin. Brush the base with a little egg white. Spoon in the pears, using a slotted spoon, and sprinkle over the nuts. Bake on the tray for 30 minutes, until golden.

3. Meanwhile, scrape the seeds from the vanilla pod into the buttery juices and simmer for a few minutes until syrupy. Discard the pod.

4. Reduce the oven temperature to 160°C/ fan 140°C/gas 3. Drizzle the tart with the syrup and bake for a further 5–10 minutes. Cool in the tin for 15 minutes before removing. Serve with vanilla ice cream.

Italian baked almond cheesecake

This is classic baked vanilla cheesecake with an
amaretti-flavoured base and almond top.

SERVES 8

TAKES 15 MINUTES, PLUS 45 MINUTES
BAKING AND OVER 1 HOUR CHILLING

200g amaretti biscuits, crushed
50g unsalted butter, melted
500g ricotta
1 vanilla pod, split lengthways
  and seeds scraped
125g golden caster sugar
250g tub mascarpone
100g ground almonds
2 tbsp cornflour
3 large free-range eggs
Grated zest of 1 lemon
Handful of flaked almonds
Icing sugar, for dusting
Cream, to serve (optional)

1. Preheat the oven to 180°C/fan 160°C/gas 4. Mix
the crushed biscuits with the melted butter, tip into
the base of a 20cm non-stick springform cake tin
and press down firmly in an even layer with a
spoon. Chill for 5–10 minutes.

2. Meanwhile, beat the ricotta, vanilla seeds, sugar,
mascarpone, almonds, cornflour, eggs and lemon
zest together in a bowl with an electric hand whisk
until smooth. Pour into the prepared tin and scatter
with the flaked almonds.

3. Place on a baking sheet and bake for 45 minutes
until golden, but still slightly wobbly in the centre.
Turn off the oven, open the door and leave the
cheesecake inside completely to cool. Chill for a
further hour or more. Then remove from the tin and
dust with icing sugar. Serve with cream, if you like.

Variation Add 150g of fresh raspberries
or blueberries to the cheesecake mixture
before baking for a fruitier version.

Free-form blackberry and apple pie

This is fantastically easy because you don't need a special dish or tin in which to make it, just a sturdy, flat baking sheet.

SERVES 6
TAKES 1 HOUR, PLUS 30 MINUTES CHILLING

200g plain flour, plus extra to dust
125g chilled unsalted butter, cubed
1 medium egg, beaten
100g golden caster sugar
3 eating apples, such as Braeburn or Cox's
300g blackberries
1 lemon, finely grated zest, plus 1 tbsp juice
25g fresh breadcrumbs

1. Whiz the flour and butter together in a food processor until the mixture resembles breadcrumbs. Add the egg and 2 tablespoons of the sugar, then whiz again until the mixture just forms a ball. Wrap the pastry in cling film and chill for 30 minutes.

2. Preheat the oven to 200°C/fan 180°C/gas 6. Quarter, core and cut the apples into chunky wedges and mix in a bowl with all but 1 teaspoon of the remaining sugar, the blackberries, lemon zest and juice.

3. Roll out the pastry on a large sheet of floured baking paper into a 30cm disc. Upturn the pastry and paper on to a baking sheet, then peel off the paper.

4. Sprinkle the centre of the pastry with breadcrumbs. Pile the prepared fruit on top, leaving a wide border free. Fold the pastry edges up and over the fruit, then sprinkle with the reserved sugar. Bake for 35–40 minutes, until the pastry is golden and the fruit tender.

Apple crumble tart

This is a delicious tart that you can bake ahead of time, and re-heat just before serving, making it ideal for entertaining.

SERVES ABOUT 6–8
TAKES 40 MINUTES, PLUS
20 MINUTES BAKING

1.5kg eating apples, such as Braeburn or Cox's
Juice of 1 small lemon
100g caster sugar
225g sheet ready-rolled puff pastry, thawed if frozen
100g plain flour
¼ tsp ground cinnamon
90g unsalted butter
50g ground almonds
50g soft brown sugar
3 tbsp melted butter
Ice cream, cream or custard, to serve

1. Preheat the oven to 190°C/fan 170°C/gas 5. Peel, core and chop half the apples into a large pan. Add the lemon juice and caster sugar and place over a high heat until the juices start to run, then cover and cook gently for 10–15 minutes, stirring, until the fruit is pulpy. Leave to cool.

2. Lay the pastry on a buttered baking sheet and prick with a fork. Bake for 10 minutes until risen, then press the layers flat using a tea towel. Bake for another 5 minutes until golden brown and crisp.

3. Meanwhile, core, peel and thinly slice the remaining apples. Whiz the flour, cinnamon, butter and almonds together into a processor until crumbly, then mix in the soft brown sugar.

4. Spread the apple purée over the pastry, right to the edges, and place the sliced apples on top. Brush them with melted butter, then sprinkle the crumble evenly on top. Bake for 20 minutes until the top is brown and crunchy. Leave to cool. Serve with ice cream, cream or custard.

Cherry pie

The trick with a fruit pie like this is the cornflour in the fruit filling, which helps to thicken the juices as it cooks.

SERVES 6
TAKES 55 MINUTES

1 tbsp cornflour
25g golden caster sugar
Pinch of ground cinnamon
500g cherries, stones removed
350g sweet shortcrust pastry
  (shop-bought or for
  homemade, see page 183)
1 tbsp milk, for brushing
2 tbsp golden granulated sugar
Cream, to serve

1. Mix the cornflour, sugar and cinnamon together in a bowl, then add the cherries and gently toss together. Put a baking sheet in the oven and preheat it to 220°C/fan 200°C/gas 7.

2. Grease a 23cm pie dish – ideally one made of enamel or metal. Roll out half the pastry and use to line the dish. Pile the cherry mixture into the centre and spoon over 4 tablespoons of water. Brush the pastry edges with water. Roll out the remaining pastry and use to cover the pie, making a hole in the centre. Press the edges to seal, trim the edges and then crimp them with your forefinger and thumb.

3. Brush the pie with milk and sprinkle with the granulated sugar. Bake on the baking sheet for 15 minutes. Then reduce the oven temperature to 180°C/fan 160°C/gas 4 and bake for a further 15–20 minutes until the pastry is pale golden. Serve with cream.

Pecan treacle tart

Treacle tart is one of the most popular puddings around, but try adding pecan nuts to the mix and just see how the best can get even better.

SERVES 8

TAKES 20 MINUTES, PLUS 1 HOUR BAKING, 45 MINUTES CHILLING AND COOLING TIME

350g sweet shortcrust pastry (shop-bought or for homemade, see page 183)
1 apple
200g shelled pecan nuts
50g butter, melted
350g golden syrup, plus 2 tbsp for drizzling
150g fresh white breadcrumbs
Zest and juice of 1 lemon
Clotted cream, to serve (optional)

1. Thinly roll out the pastry and use to line a 23-cm round loose-bottomed, fluted tart tin. Chill for 45 minutes.

2. Preheat the oven to 180°C/fan 160°C/gas 4. Line the pastry with baking paper and cover with a layer of baking beans. Bake blind for 15 minutes. Remove the paper and beans and bake for a further 5 minutes, until pale golden.

3. Peel, core and grate the apple. Finely chop half the pecans. In a bowl, mix together the butter, golden syrup, breadcrumbs, lemon zest and juice, grated apple and chopped pecans. Spoon the mixture into the pastry case and arrange the remaining whole pecans on top. Bake for 40 minutes. Remove from the oven and leave to cool slightly.

4. Remove the tart from the tin and cut into slices. Drizzle with the extra golden syrup and serve with clotted cream, if you like.

★ DELICIOUS. TIP If you don't have a sweet tooth, you could use plain shortcrust pastry instead of sweet shortcrust pastry.

Variation This tart also works well with shelled walnuts instead of pecans.

Creamy coconut, cherry and lime tart

This tart is so simple to make, you could even serve it up as a mid-week treat.

SERVES 8

TAKES 25 MINUTES, PLUS 1 HOUR CHILLING

100g butter

200g coconut biscuits, finely crushed

284ml carton double cream

150ml sweetened condensed milk

Finely grated zest and juice of 4 limes

6 tsp red cherry conserve

1. Melt the butter in a small saucepan. Add the biscuits and stir well. Press into the base and up the sides of a 20cm round x 3cm deep loose-bottomed, fluted flan tin using the back of a spoon. Chill for 20 minutes.

2. Pour the cream into a large bowl and stir in the condensed milk, lime zest and juice. Whisk with an electric hand whisk until thick. Pour into the tin and level the top. Drop spoonfuls of the conserve into the filling and swirl with a skewer to create a pattern. Chill for at least 1 hour before serving.

Mango tartes Tatins

These are a clever but simple variation of the classic apple tarte Tatin, and they are just as delicious.

SERVES 6

TAKES 50 MINUTES, PLUS 15 MINUTES CHILLING

40g butter, plus extra to grease
3 small ripe mangoes, peeled
50g golden granulated sugar
375g pack ready-rolled puff pastry
Whipped cream, to serve (optional)

1. Base line 6cm x 8cm individual round tartlet tins with baking paper and grease the sides with butter. Cut away the flesh from either side of each mango stone in one piece. Cut each cheek lengthways into 10 slices, leaving the slices joined together at the top.

2. Gently heat the sugar in a large, heavy-based frying pan until it dissolves and turns brown. Stir in the butter, then add the mango pieces, curved side down, and cook for 2–3 minutes, pressing down on them to fan out the slices. Lift the mango into the tins, curved-side down, and drizzle with any remaining caramel.

3. Unroll the pastry and, using a tin as a guide, cut out 6 rounds. Use to cover each mango piece. Chill for at least 15 minutes.

4. Preheat the oven to 220°C/fan 200°C/gas 7. Bake for 20–25 minutes until the pastry is puffed up and golden. Carefully invert on to plates and serve with whipped cream, if you like.

Mincemeat shortcake slice

Don't reserve mincemeat just for Christmas: treat yourself
and make this wonderful tart at any time of the year.

SERVES 6
TAKES 1 HOUR 45 MINUTES, PLUS
CHILLING

250g unsalted butter, softened
90g golden or white icing sugar,
  plus extra to dust
1½ tsp vanilla extract
250g plain flour
600g good-quality mincemeat
Cream, to serve

1. Put the butter, icing sugar and vanilla into a
bowl, and cream together with an electric hand
whisk until pale and fluffy. Sift over the flour and a
pinch of salt, and mix until smooth. Press some of
the shortcake mixture into the base of 35cm x 11cm
tranche tin to make a 3mm-thick layer. Spoon the
rest into a piping bag fitted with a 1cm star nozzle
and pipe a layer along the inside edges of the tin.
Freeze for 10 minutes.

2. Preheat the oven to 190°C/fan 170°C/gas 5,
and put in a baking sheet to heat up. Spoon the
mincemeat into the shortcake case. Pipe the
remaining shortcake on top in a diamond pattern.
You can cover it and freeze for up to 1 month at
this point.

3. Bake on the hot baking sheet for 30–35 minutes,
or until golden. Cool slightly in the tin, then
carefully remove. Serve warm in slices, dusted
with icing sugar and drizzled with cream.

★ DELICIOUS. TIP You can assemble this tart in
advance, then freeze, unbaked and covered in
cling film, for up to 1 month. Defrost at room
temperature then bake as indicated in step 3 above.

Raspberry meringue pie

This fabulous recipe offers you the taste of summer in every mouthful. Use the freshest raspberries you can find.

SERVES 8

TAKES 50 MINUTES, PLUS ABOUT 35 MINUTES BAKING, 30 MINUTES CHILLING AND COOLING TIME

300g sweet shortcrust pastry (shop-bought or for homemade, see page 183)

For the raspberry filling:
800g raspberries
5 tbsp cornflour
100–125g golden caster sugar, to taste
2 tbsp fresh lemon juice
5 large egg yolks
60g butter

For the meringue topping:
3 large egg whites
175g golden caster sugar

1. Make a 25cm pastry case that is 4cm deep with the pastry and bake it blind (see page 184). Then reduce the oven temperature to 180°C/ fan 160°C/gas 4.

2. Make the filling. Whiz the raspberries into a purée in a food processor, then pass through a sieve into a pan to remove the seeds.

3. Mix the cornflour, 100g of the sugar, the lemon juice and 1 tablespoon of water together in a small bowl into a paste. Mix into the purée and stir over a medium heat until just boiling. Simmer for 1 minute, stirring, until thickened. Add the extra sugar if the raspberries are too tart. Remove from the heat and beat in the egg yolks and butter. Cool slightly, then pour into the pastry case and chill for 30 minutes.

4. Make the topping. Whisk the egg whites to soft peaks, then gradually whisk in the sugar to make a stiff, glossy meringue. Pile on top of the chilled filling and bake for 8–10 minutes, or until pale golden. Serve immediately.

★ DELICIOUS. TIP This pie is best served fresh from the oven, so the juice from the filling doesn't soak into the crisp pastry shell and make it soggy.

Variation You could also make this with fresh blackberries in autumn, when they're in season.

Passion fruit and lemon brulée tart

This zingy tart is something quite special, so serve it for a celebratory occasion.

SERVES 10–12
TAKES 35 MINUTES, PLUS ABOUT 1 HOUR BAKING AND COOLING

350g sweet shortcrust pastry (shop-bought or for homemade, see page 183)
3 ripe (wrinkly) passion fruit
Juice and finely grated zest of 2 large lemons
6 medium eggs
250g caster sugar
142ml carton double cream
Icing sugar, for dusting
Passion fruit sorbet, to serve (optional)

1. Make a 25cm pastry case that is 4cm deep with the pastry (see page 184). Preheat the oven to 120°C/fan 100°C/gas ½.

2. Halve each passion fruit and scoop the pulp into a sieve set over a measuring jug. Rub through with a wooden spoon to get about 50ml juice. Discard the seeds. Add enough lemon juice to make up to 175ml.

3. Whisk the eggs and sugar together lightly in a bowl with a fork. Stir in the fruit-juice mixture and cream. Pour through a sieve back into the jug, then stir in the lemon zest. Pour into the pastry case and bake for 45–50 minutes, or until just set but slightly wobbly in the centre. Leave to cool, but don't chill.

4. Just before serving, remove the tart from the tin and dust with icing sugar. Caramelise it using a blowtorch until it turns deep golden. Cool and serve slices with passion fruit sorbet, if you like.

★ DELICIOUS. TIP This tart is best filled, baked and eaten on the day it's made. Serve it at room temperature, not chilled.

Orange cream cheese flans with chocolate

These sophisticated tarts are not only yummy, but they're sure to impress your guests.

MAKES 6

TAKES 40 MINUTES, ABOUT 30 MIN-UTES BAKING, PLUS COOLING

375g sweet shortcrust pastry (shop-bought or for homemade, see page 183)
250g cream cheese
Zest of 1 medium orange
1 tbsp caster sugar
142ml carton double cream
1 large whole egg
3 medium eggs, separated
150g plain chocolate
6 physalis (Cape gooseberries)
Icing sugar, for dusting

1. Preheat the oven to 200°C/fan 180°C/gas 6. Line 6cm x 9cm-round loose-bottomed flan tins with the pastry and bake blind (see page 184).

2. Reduce the oven temperature to 160°C/fan 140°C/gas 3. Beat the cream cheese with the orange zest and sugar, then slowly mix in the cream until smooth. Mix in the whole egg and egg yolks. In a clean bowl, whisk the egg whites into soft peaks. Carefully fold into the cheese mixture. Divide equally among the pastry cases and bake for 18–20 minutes until golden. Cool for 30 minutes, remove from the tins and leave to go cold.

3. Melt the chocolate in a bowl set over a pan of simmering water. Spoon two-thirds into a greaseproof-paper piping bag, snip off the end and drizzle over the top of each flan. Fold back the husk of each physalis and dip the fruit into the remaining chocolate. Leave to set on greaseproof paper. Decorate each flan with a physalis, dust with icing sugar and serve.

classic british
puddings

Pear and blackberry cobbler

A cobbler is halfway between a crumble and a pie – the best of
both worlds.

SERVES 6

TAKES 1 HOUR

500g pears, peeled, cored and
  cut into wedges

400g blackberries

200g golden caster sugar

½ tsp ground cinnamon

1 tbsp cornflour

175g self-raising flour

75g chilled unsalted butter,
  cubed

125ml buttermilk or wholemilk
  natural yogurt

Cream, to serve

1. Preheat the oven to 200°C/fan 180°C/gas 6. Pile
the pears and blackberries into an ovenproof dish
about 26cm x 18cm. Sprinkle over 50g of the sugar,
the cinnamon and cornflour. Gently stir together
to mix.

2. Put the flour in a food processor, add the butter
and 100g of the sugar, and whiz for a few seconds
until the mixture resembles fine breadcrumbs.
Add the buttermilk or yogurt and whiz very briefly
until a squidgy dough forms.

3. Scatter clumps of the dough over the fruit
– don't cover completely. Sprinkle over the rest of
the sugar and bake for 40 minutes, or until the
fruit is tender and the topping cooked through and
pale golden. Serve hot with cream.

Variation Swap the pears for apples and the
blackberries for raspberries. These are also
absolutely delicious together.

Eccles cake baked apples

In a clever twist, the spicy, fruity filling from Eccles cakes is used here to stuff baked apples instead.

SERVES 4

TAKES 15 MINUTES, 40–45 MINUTES IN THE OVEN, PLUS COOLING

4 large Bramley apples (about 300g each)
Custard, thick cream or vanilla ice cream, to serve

For the fruity filling:
50g butter
50g light muscovado sugar
50g dark muscovado sugar
250g currants
1 tsp ground allspice
1 tsp freshly grated nutmeg
½ tsp ground cinnamon
Pinch of ground cloves
Finely grated zest of 1 lemon and 1 tbsp juice

1. Make the filling. Melt the butter in a pan, add both sugars, remove from the heat and stir to remove any lumps. Stir in the currants, spices, lemon zest and juice. Leave to cool.

2. Preheat the oven to 180°C/fan 160°C/gas 4. Core the apples using an apple corer then open up the cavities until they measure about 3cm across. Slice a little off the base of each apple so they sit flat, then score through the skin, horizontally around the middle of each one. This should stop them bursting in the oven.

3. Place the apples in a shallow baking dish and generously fill the cavities with the filling, piling any excess on top. Spoon 2 tablespoons of water into the dish and bake in the oven for 20 minutes. Remove the dish from the oven and cover loosely with foil. Bake for a further 20–25 minutes or until the apples are soft right through to the centre. Serve immediately with the juices from the dish and some custard, thick cream or vanilla ice cream.

★ DELICIOUS. TIP These apples should be served immediately, as they will collapse if left to stand.

Stem ginger and dark muscovado puddings

These taste like sticky gingerbread, but cooking them as individual puddings makes for a smarter-looking dessert.

SERVES 6

TAKES 40 MINUTES, PLUS 20 MINUTES IN THE OVEN

150g softened butter, plus extra for greasing

240g stem ginger from a jar, plus 4 tbsp of the syrup

175g dark muscovado sugar

315ml double cream

175g plain flour

½ tsp ground ginger

½ tsp baking powder

½ rounded tsp bicarbonate of soda

2 medium eggs, beaten

2 tbsp molasses sugar

1. Preheat the oven to 200°C/fan 180°C/gas 6 and put a baking sheet on the middle shelf. Lightly grease 6 x 120ml non-stick pudding moulds with butter.

2. Put the stem ginger and its syrup into a food processor, and whiz until finely chopped but not completely smooth. Spoon 120g of the ginger into a small pan and add 75g of the muscovado sugar, half the butter and 200ml of the double cream. Set aside.

3. Sift the flour, ground ginger, baking powder and bicarbonate of soda into a mixing bowl. Add the eggs, the remaining butter and muscovado sugar. Mix the molasses sugar with 1 tablespoon of cream and add to the bowl. Beat together until smooth. Whisk in 150ml of warm water and the remaining whizzed ginger.

4. Spoon the mixture evenly into the moulds, put on to the hot baking sheet and bake for 20 minutes. Meanwhile, stir the ginger sauce over a low heat until heated through. Turn the puddings out on to six warmed plates, pour over the sauce and serve with the remaining cream.

Pineapple upside-down cake

You can serve this comforting upside-down cake either warm as a dessert with lashings of custard or cream, or cold as a cake for afternoon tea.

SERVES 6
TAKES 20 MINUTES, 35–40 MINUTES BAKING, PLUS 30 MINUTES COOLING

300g unsalted butter, plus extra for greasing
250g golden syrup
6 fresh or canned pineapple rings
6 glacé cherries
300g caster sugar
4 medium eggs, lightly beaten
300g self-raising flour
6–8 tbsp milk

1. Preheat the oven to 180°C/fan 160°C/gas 4. Grease and line a deep 30cm x 23cm baking dish or roasting tin with baking paper. Pour the golden syrup into the tin, pop in the oven and heat for 2 minutes. Tilt the tin to spread out the syrup evenly. Top with the pineapple rings and put a glacé cherry into the middle of each one.

2. In a large bowl, cream the butter and sugar until fluffy. Gradually beat in the eggs until combined, then fold in the flour and enough milk to make a smooth consistency. Spoon the mixture into the tin, making sure that the surface is level. Bake for 35–40 minutes, or until golden. To test, insert a skewer into the centre – it should come out clean. Leave to cool in the tin for 30 minutes.

3. Carefully invert the tin on to a chopping board. Cut the cake into slices and serve warm or at room temperature.

Variation Replace the pineapple and cherries with thickly sliced apples or pears, and a scattering of shredded stem ginger.

Lemon syllabub and passion fruit trifle

Trifle has never tasted so exotic. The unique flavour and sweetness of passion fruit permeates this glam dessert.

SERVES 8–10
TAKES 40 MINUTES, PLUS COOLING AND CHILLING

8 trifle sponges
4 tbsp good-quality lemon curd
4 tbsp limoncello
6 ripe passion fruit, halved
Edible silver balls, to decorate

For the custard:
284ml double cream
300ml full-cream milk
Pared zest of 1 lemon
6 large egg yolks
1 tbsp cornflour
50g caster sugar

For the syllabub:
568ml double cream
50g caster sugar
Finely grated zest of 1 small
  lemon, plus 25ml juice
75ml dry white wine, chilled

1. Make the custard. Bring the cream, milk and lemon zest to the boil in a non-stick pan. Set aside for 20 minutes. Lightly whisk the egg yolks, cornflour and sugar together in a bowl. Bring the milk back to the boil, then slowly mix into the yolks. Strain back into a clean pan and cook over a low heat for 5 minutes, until thickened – don't boil. Pour into a bowl, cover the surface with cling film and cool.

2. Meanwhile, split the sponges in half and spread with the lemon curd. Cut each into four and put into a 2-litre glass serving bowl. Drizzle over the limoncello. Scoop out the passion-fruit pulp on to the trifle sponges. Pour over the cold custard, cover and chill for 3–4 hours, or overnight.

3. The next day, make the syllabub. Whisk the cream, sugar, lemon zest, lemon juice and wine together until the mixture just holds its shape. Spoon over the trifle and chill for at least 1 hour. Decorate with the silver balls just before serving.

★ DELICIOUS. TIP For the decoration, we used edible sugar dragées in three sizes, or use any edible silver balls.

Dorset apple cake

There are as many versions of this cake as there are cooks, but this lemony one is wonderful. Serve with clotted cream.

SERVES 8
TAKES 25 MINUTES, 1 HOUR BAKING, PLUS COOLING

225g butter, softened, plus extra for greasing
450g Bramley apples
Finely grated zest and juice of 1 lemon
225g caster sugar, plus extra for dredging
3 large eggs
225g self-raising flour
2 tsp baking powder
25g ground almonds
1 tbsp demerara sugar
Clotted cream, to serve

1. Preheat the oven to 180°C/fan 160°C/gas 4. Grease a deep 24cm springform cake tin and line with baking paper. Peel, core and cut the apples into 1cm pieces, and toss with the lemon juice.

2. Beat together the butter, caster sugar and lemon zest in a bowl until pale and fluffy. Beat in the eggs, one at a time, adding a little flour with each egg.

3. Sift the remaining flour and the baking powder into the bowl, and fold in with the ground almonds. Drain the apple pieces well, then stir into the mixture. Spoon into the prepared tin, lightly level the top and sprinkle with the demerara sugar. Bake for 1 hour or until a skewer inserted into the centre of the cake comes out clean. If the cake starts to look too brown, cover with a sheet of baking paper after about 45 minutes.

4. Leave the cake to cool in the tin for 10 minutes, then remove and dredge heavily with the extra caster sugar. Cut into wedges and serve warm with clotted cream.

Variation Though it's not traditional in Dorset, firm pears such as Conference would also work well in this pudding.

Jam roly-poly

As this pud is made with suet it has a wonderful nostalgic quality to it. You can steam or bake it, but either way it's simple to make. Serve with custard.

SERVES 6
TAKES 10 MINUTES, PLUS
30–40 MINUTES BAKING

Butter, for greasing
150g self-raising flour, plus extra for dusting
2 tbsp caster sugar
75g vegetable suet
100ml milk
150g blackberry, black cherry or blueberry jam
Custard, to serve

1. Preheat the oven to 200°C/fan 180°C/gas 6. Grease a sheet of baking paper and lay it greased-side up.

2. Sift the flour into a bowl and stir in the sugar, suet and a pinch of salt. Add the milk and mix to a firm dough.

3. Roll out on a lightly floured surface to form a rectangle about 20cm x 30cm. Spread thickly with the jam. Roll up tightly from the short end and pinch the ends to seal, then carefully transfer to the greased baking paper, seam-side down. Wrap in the greased baking paper, then wrap a sheet of foil around the baking paper, twisting the ends to seal.

4. Sit the roly-poly package on a wire rack set inside a roasting tin and fill the tin with boiling water, making sure that the water does not touch the foil. Bake for 35–40 minutes. Remove the foil and baking paper and serve slices of the pudding with custard.

Variation Change the jam to suit your mood, or to what you have available. Even marmalade is delicious, especially if the custard is flavoured with orange zest.

Sticky toffee pudding

Luscious, sticky and irresistible, steamed puddings are one of Britain's greatest culinary gifts to the world, and this classic recipe is no exception.

MAKES 6 INDIVIDUAL PUDDINGS
TAKES 25 MINUTES, 15–18 MINUTES
BAKING, PLUS COOLING

85g softened unsalted butter,
  plus extra for greasing
225g soft Medjool dates, pitted
  and coarsely chopped
100ml dark rum
175g plain flour
1 tsp baking powder
1 tsp bicarbonate of soda
150g dark muscovado sugar
2 large eggs

For the sauce:
300ml double cream
200g dark muscovado sugar
60g unsalted butter
50ml dark rum

1. Preheat the oven to 180°C/fan 160°C/gas 4. Butter 6 x 200ml individual pudding moulds.

2. Put the dates, rum and 100ml of boiling water into a small pan, and simmer for 5 minutes, stirring occasionally, until the dates are very soft. Cool.

3. Sift the flour, baking powder, bicarbonate of soda and a pinch of salt into a bowl. In another bowl, beat the butter and sugar together with an electric hand whisk for 2 minutes, until creamy. Beat in the eggs, one at a time. Alternately stir in the flour mixture and the dates, a little at a time.

4. Divide the pudding mix among the moulds, then bake for 15–18 minutes or until a skewer inserted into each cake comes out clean. Cool for 5 minutes, then turn out on to serving plates.

5. Meanwhile, make the toffee sauce. Bring the cream, sugar and butter to the boil in a small pan. Simmer for 3 minutes, add the rum and cook for a further minute. Pour over the puddings and serve immediately.

★ DELICIOUS. TIP You can freeze the puddings and sauce separately for up to 3 months. Defrost completely, then re-heat the puddings at 180°C/fan160°C/gas 4 for 8–10 minutes, and the sauce in a pan.

Syrupy marmalade steamed pudding

If you thought steamed puddings were heavy and stodgy, this light and airy marmalade pud will help change your mind.

SERVES 4–6
TAKES 20 MINUTES, PLUS 1½ HOURS STEAMING

100g softened butter, plus extra for greasing
125ml golden syrup
Zest and juice (100ml) of 2 oranges
100g caster sugar
2 large eggs, at room temperature
2 tbsp orange marmalade
100g self-raising flour
50ml milk

1. Grease a 1-litre pudding basin. Put 2 tablespoons of the golden syrup and 2 teaspoons of orange zest into the base.

2. Beat the butter and sugar together until pale and creamy. Beat in the eggs, one at a time, followed by the marmalade. Sift over half the flour and gently fold in. Add a little milk to loosen, then sift over and mix in the remaining flour and milk until you have a soft dropping consistency.

3. Spoon into the basin and cover with a disc of buttered baking paper (butter-side down). Cover with pleated foil and tie in place with string.

4. Steam for 1½ hours, adding more hot water when necessary to prevent the pan boiling dry.

5. Meanwhile, make the marmalade sauce. Put the remaining golden syrup and orange zest and the orange juice into a small pan, and simmer for 5–6 minutes, until thick and syrupy.

6. Turn the pudding out on to a serving plate, pour over the sauce and serve.

★ DELICIOUS. TIP Make sure the eggs and butter are at room temperature before using, as this will prevent the mixture from curdling.

Eve's pudding

Named after Eve, this biblical pud naturally features apples, which stew in their own juices under a delicious vanilla sponge.

SERVES 4

TAKES 15 MINUTES, PLUS 40 MINUTES BAKING

600g cooking apples, peeled, cored and roughly chopped
75g light muscovado sugar
Grated zest and juice of 1 lemon
¼ tsp ground cinnamon
100g butter
100g caster sugar, plus extra for dusting
2 large eggs
½ tsp vanilla extract
100g self-raising flour

1. Preheat the oven to 180°C/fan 160°C/gas 4. Put the apples in a large bowl and toss with the sugar, lemon zest, lemon juice and cinnamon. Transfer to a round or oval, shallow 2-litre ovenproof dish and set aside.

2. Beat the butter and caster sugar together in a bowl until pale and fluffy. Beat in the eggs, one at a time. Mix in the vanilla, then sift over the flour and gently mix to make a dropping consistency.

3. Spread the mixture over the apples and bake for 40 minutes or until the topping is cooked through and golden. Sprinkle with extra caster sugar and serve hot with custard.

★ DELICIOUS. TIP You can freeze this pudding for up to 3 months. Defrost thoroughly before re-heating at 180°C/fan 160°C/gas 4 for 8–10 minutes.

Queen of puddings

This is a layered baked pudding, with a lemon-flavoured bread and custard base, jam filling and a crisp meringue topping. Perfect for Sunday lunch.

SERVES 6
TAKES 20 MINUTES, PLUS 25 MINUTES BAKING

50g unsalted butter, softened, plus extra for greasing
125g caster sugar
Finely grated zest of 1 lemon
600ml milk
150g fresh white breadcrumbs
4 large eggs, separated, plus 1 extra egg white
4 tbsp raspberry jam

1. Preheat the oven to 180°C/fan 160°C/gas 4. Butter a shallow 1-litre ovenproof dish or 6 x 300ml individual dishes.

2. Bring the butter, 25g of the sugar, the lemon zest, milk and a pinch of salt to a gentle simmer in a pan. Add the breadcrumbs and remove from the heat, stirring often until thickened – about 15 minutes. Then stir in the egg yolks and spoon into the prepared dish/dishes. Bake for 15 minutes or until just set.

3. Heat the jam in a small pan until runny. Carefully spread over the top of the baked mixture, taking care not to break the surface.

4. Put the egg whites and remaining sugar into a heatproof bowl. Place over a pan of simmering water and whisk for 4 minutes until the sugar has dissolved and the whites have formed soft peaks. Swirl over the top of the pudding to form peaks. Bake for 10 minutes, or until the meringue has set and is lightly browned and crisp. Serve at once.

Variation Try apricot or peach jam instead, or use fine-cut marmalade and flavour the milk and breadcrumb mixture with a little finely grated orange zest before baking.

Pecan banoffee pie

This is an excellent pudding for when time is short, because it uses a ready-made pastry case; if you want to make one yourself, see pages 182–3.

SERVES 6–8
READY IN 15 MINUTES

350g ready-made toffee sauce, such as dulce de leche

20cm sweet pastry case (shop-bought or see page 183 for recipe)

3 ripe bananas, sliced

Good handful of pecan nuts, roughly chopped

284ml carton double cream

2 tbsp Marsala

Plain chocolate, grated, to decorate

1. Spread half the toffee sauce over the bottom of the pastry case and scatter with the sliced bananas and half of the pecans. Spread with the remaining toffee sauce.

2. Whip the cream to soft peaks and fold in the Marsala. Spoon the cream over the toffee and bananas.

3. Sprinkle with the remaining pecans and the grated chocolate, and serve cut into wedges.

Apple and cinnamon fritters

These are very naughty, but very nice. Just make sure you serve them straight away while they are hot and crisp.

SERVES 4
READY IN 15 MINUTES

Sunflower oil, for deep frying
1 tsp ground cinnamon
1 tbsp plain flour
3 small eating apples
Caster sugar, for dusting
Whipped cream, for serving

For the batter:
1 egg, separated
75ml good-quality cider
75g plain flour

1. Make the batter. In a large bowl, whisk the egg yolk with the cider, then gradually beat into the flour to form a smooth batter. In a separate bowl, whisk the egg white into soft peaks, then carefully fold into the batter.

2. Pour the sunflower oil into a deep saucepan and heat until a cube of bread dropped into the oil turns golden in about 5 seconds.

3. Mix the cinnamon and flour together. Peel, core and cut each apple into 8 wedges. Dust with the spiced flour, then dip in the batter. Cook the apples in the hot oil for 2–3 minutes, until crisp and golden. Remove with a slotted spoon and drain on kitchen paper.

4. Divide among warmed plates and dust with caster sugar. Serve with a bowl of whipped cream.

Variation To make this for children, replace the cider with apple juice.

How to make a pastry case

1. Lightly grease your loose-bottomed flan tin with a little butter. If you are using chilled pastry, re-knead it briefly on a lightly floured surface until smooth. Roll out the pastry thinly on a lightly floured surface, using a lightly floured rolling pin, into a round that is 5cm larger all the way round than your tin. Turn the pastry as you go to keep it circular, and use short, little strokes – do not stretch the pastry or it will shrink during cooking.

2. Fold the pastry over the rolling pin and carefully lift it over your tart tin, making sure there is roughly an equal amount overhanging the edges on all sides. Gently ease the pastry down into the bottom of the tin, then press it up against the sides. Roll the rolling pin over the top to cut off the excess pastry, then press into the little grooves using your index finger.

3. Prick the base here and there with a fork; this will help prevent the base from rising during cooking. Chill in the fridge for 20 minutes. Preheat the oven to 200°C/fan 180°C/gas 6.

4. Line the chilled pastry case with a sheet of crumpled greaseproof paper that is large enough to cover the top edges, tucking it down well into the corners. Then cover the base with a thin layer of baking beans, making sure they go right up to the sides. (Use ceramic ones, or some dried red kidney beans.)

5. Bake the pastry case for 12–15 minutes until the edges are starting to go biscuit coloured. Carefully remove the paper and beans, and return the case to the oven for 4 minutes. Remove once more and brush the base lightly with a little beaten egg white. This will help to keep the pastry crisp and seal up any little holes to prevent it leaking. Return the pastry case to the oven for a further 3–4 minutes until crisp and golden.

Sweet shortcrust pastry

Perfect for all sorts of pies and desserts.

MAKES ENOUGH TO LINE A 25CM,
LOOSE-BOTTOMED TART TIN THAT IS
4CM DEEP

175g plain flour
A small pinch of salt
50g icing sugar
100g chilled lightly salted
  butter, cut into small pieces
1 medium egg yolk
2 tsp cold water

1. Sift the flour, salt and icing sugar together into a food processor or mixing bowl. Add the butter and either whiz in the processor or rub together with your fingertips until the mixture looks like fine breadcrumbs.

2. Mix the egg yolk with the cold water. If you have used a food processor, tip the 'crumbs' into a bowl and stir in enough of the egg-yolk mixture until everything comes together into a ball.

3. Turn out on to a lightly floured surface and knead briefly until smooth. The pastry is now ready to be used or chilled. If using straight away, roll it out and then chill for 20 minutes before cooking to allow the pastry to 'rest'. This helps to stop it shrinking. If you wish to chill the pastry for use later on, wrap it in clingfilm first. Before using, bring it back to room temperature and then re-knead briefly.

Rich shortcrust pastry

This recipe will give you a pastry that is a little more short
than usual, which makes it perfect for desserts.

MAKES ENOUGH TO LINE A 25CM,
LOOSE-BOTTOMED TART TIN THAT IS
4CM DEEP

225g plain flour
½ tsp salt
**65g chilled butter, cut into
  small pieces**
**65g chilled lard or white
  vegetable shortening, cut into
  small pieces**

1. Sift the flour and salt together into a food
processor or mixing bowl. Add the butter and lard,
and either whiz in the processor or rub together
with your fingertips until the mixture looks like fine
breadcrumbs. Sprinkle over 2 tablespoons of cold
water and process very briefly using the pulse
button or mix together with a round-bladed knife
until the mixture comes together into a ball.

2. Turn the pastry out on to a lightly floured surface
and knead briefly until smooth. The pastry is now
ready to be used or chilled.

3. If using straight away, roll it out and then chill
for 20 minutes before cooking to allow the pastry to
'rest'. This helps to stop it shrinking. If you wish to
chill the pastry for use later on, wrap it in clingfilm
first. Before using, bring it back to room
temperature and then re-knead briefly.

Custard

MAKES 600ML

1 vanilla pod (optional)
600ml full-cream milk
4 large egg yolks
4 tbsp caster sugar
3 tbsp cornflour

1. Slit open the vanilla pod, if using, and scrape out the seeds with the tip of a small knife. Put the milk, vanilla pod and seeds into a non-stick pan and bring to the boil. Remove from the heat and set aside for 20 minutes.

2. Cream the egg yolks, sugar and cornflour together in a bowl until smooth. Bring the milk back to the boil, remove the vanilla pod, if necessary, and gradually stir the milk into the egg-yolk mixture.

3. Return the mixture to the cleaned pan and cook over a medium–low heat, stirring constantly with a wooden spoon, until the custard thickens enough to coat the back of the spoon – but don't let it boil. This should take about 8 minutes. Test it by running a finger through the custard on the spoon: if it leaves a straight, clear line, it's ready. Serve hot.

★ DELICIOUS. TIP Custard must be cooked slowly over a very low heat and stirred constantly, until it gradually thickens to the point where it coats the back of a wooden spoon. Boiling point is the enemy once you have added the eggs, so always keep the temperature of the custard just below the boil. If it boils, the eggs will begin to separate, much as they would if you were making scrambled eggs. If this happens, you may be able to save the custard by quickly straining the egg mixture through a sieve into a blender and whizzing it until smooth. You may then re-heat it with a little extra blended cornflour and milk to help it stabilise, but all this will depend on how far it has curdled in the first place. So the golden rule is: don't be tempted to increase the heat.

Crème anglaise

MAKES 600ML

1 vanilla pod
450ml full-cream milk
150ml double cream
5 large egg yolks
3–4 tbsp caster sugar

1. Slit open the vanilla pod and scrape out the seeds with the tip of a small knife. Put the milk, cream, vanilla pod and seeds into a non-stick pan and bring to the boil. Remove from the heat and set aside for 20 minutes.

2. Beat the egg yolks and sugar together in a bowl until pale and creamy. Bring the milk back to the boil, remove the vanilla pod, and gradually stir the milk into the yolks.

3. Return the mixture to the cleaned pan and cook over a medium–low heat, stirring all the time with a wooden spoon, until the mixture is thick enough lightly to coat the back of the spoon – but don't let it boil. This should take about 8 minutes. Test it by running a finger through the custard on the spoon: if it leaves a straight, clear line, it's ready. Serve warm.

Vanilla ice cream

MAKES 1.2 LITRES

2 vanilla pods
500ml full-cream milk
6 egg yolks
200g caster sugar
500ml single or double cream
1 tsp vanilla extract

1. Slit open the vanilla pods and scrape out the seeds with the tip of a knife. Put the milk, vanilla pods and seeds into a non-stick pan and bring to the boil, then remove from heat and set aside for 30 minutes to infuse the milk with the flavour of the vanilla.

2. Put the egg yolks and caster sugar into a large bowl, and using an electric hand whisk, whisk for 3 minutes until pale and moussey. Bring the milk back to the boil, strain on to the egg-yolk mixture and mix until well combined.

3. Return to the cleaned-out pan and cook over a medium–low heat, stirring, for 3–4 minutes, until the mixture lightly coats the back of a wooden spoon – but do not let the mixture boil, or it will curdle. Remove from heat and set aside to cool slightly, then stir in the cream and vanilla extract. Chill until cold.

4. Pour the chilled mixture into a shallow, freezerproof container and freeze until almost, but not quite, firm. Scrape the mixture either into a bowl or a food processor and beat until smooth, then return to the container and freeze once more. Repeat this process 2–3 times, until very smooth, then leave until frozen. Or churn the mixture in an ice-cream maker, if you have one. Return to the freezerproof container, cover and freeze until required.

Index

Picture and recipe credits

Harper Collins and delicious. would like to thank the following for providing photographs:

Cristian Barnett p81; Steve Baxter p25, p45, p55, p57, p65, p67, p113, p159, p163, p167; Peter Cassidy p15, p17, p19, p21, p31, p75, p91, p93, p95, p115, p117, p119, p123, p133, p153, p161, p165; Jean Cazals p77, p85, p87, p89, p97, p101, p147; Stephen Conroy p141; Ewen Francis, p37, p79; Jonathan Gregson p49, p83, p111; Richard Jung p23, p33, p35, p51, p53, p61, p121, p149, p169, p171, p173, p175, p177; Emma Lee p63; Simon Page-Ritchie p43, p178, p181; Lis Parsons p27, p47, p73, p139, p145;

Michael Paul p41, p59, p137, p143, p151; Claire Richardson p29, p135, p157; Lucinda Symons p13; Kate Whitaker p71, p105, p107, p109, p125, p129, p131; Rob White p103

With thanks, too, for the following for creating the recipes for delicious. used in this book:

Felicity Barnum Bobb p24, p26, p28, p46, p134, p138, p156; Kate Belcher p58, p72, p102; Angela Boggiano p44, p70, p104, p106, p108, p120, p128, p168, p170, p172, p174, p176; Angela Boggiano, Alice Hart and Hannah Miles p22, p32, p34; Lorna Brash p142; Matthew Drennan p12, p60, p76, p144, p148;

Silvana Franco p62, p74, p132; Brian Glover p40; Alice Hart p66; Diana Henry p50; Catherine Hill p140; Debbie Major p30, p54, p56, p64, p82, p90, p92, p112, p114, p116, p118, p158, p160, p164, p166; Tom Norrington-Davies and John Topham p80; Meena Pathak and Sunil Menon p94, p122; Carol Tennant p52; Linda Tubby p14, p16, p18, p20, p78, p84, p86, p88, p96, p152; Marcus Wareing p136, p162; Kate Weatherall p124, p130; Jenny White p42, p178, p180; Mitzie Wilson p48, p110; Mitzie Wilson and Debbie Major p150